4 Wheeler's Guide Trails of the TAHOE NATIONAL FOREST

D1571532

William C. Teie

Deer Valley Press
Rescue, California

Produced and published by:

Deer Valley Press

5125 Deer Valley Road
Rescue, CA 95672
(530) 676-7401
www.deervalleypress.com

About Deer Valley Press - Deer Valley Press was established in 1993 to develop and publish training materials for the wildland firefighter. It's two primary products, both award-winning, are the ***Firefighter's Handbook on Wildland Firefighting*** published in 1994 and the ***Fire Officer's Handbook on Wildland Firefighting*** published in 1997. In May 2000, ***Fundamentals of Wildland Firefighting*** was published.

In January 1998, Deer Valley Press published its first four-wheeler's guide, ***4 Wheeler's Guide to the Rubicon Trail.*** In 1999, ***4 Wheeler's Guide Trails of the San Bernardino Mountains*** was published.

Library of Congress Catalog Card Number 00-190061
ISBN 0-9640709-7-9

First printed in April 2001
10 9 8 7 6 5 4 3 2 1

Printed in China

How to Use this Guide

This Guide is intended to make your visit to the trails of the Tahoe National Forest a memorable experience. The Guide includes important information and historical facts, maps, and photographs.

Use this Guide to:

Plan your trip - Traveling the trails of the Tahoe National Forest is not a trip for the unprepared. Refer to the Guide for helpful hints on what to do before you venture out into the great outdoors. The checklists found in the section on trip logistic should help remind you of important pre-trip details. The maps can be used to plan your trip, and the contact lists located in the appendix can help you contact various agencies for more information and/or permits.

Guide your trip - The maps included in the Guide will help direct you along the way. The descriptive information will give you an appreciation for the history of the area and the challenges and pleasures of the experience.

Remember your trip - One of the most important functions of the Guide is to aid in recalling your great adventure and to show others what you "went through."

This Guide is not a training manual on how to operate four-wheel drive vehicles in tough terrain. Those are skills that can't be learned from books, but from "on-the-job training" on the trail and with experienced mentors.

Acknowledgements

There are many people that need to be acknowledged for their assistance in the development of this Guide. The two most important people were **Glenn Sundstrom** of the Tahoe National Forest who provided invaluable information regarding each of the trails and the history of the area, and **Bob Reed**, the "head wagon master" of the Sierra Trek event. Others that were of assistance were **Doug Pewitt** and **Phil Sexton** of the Tahoe National Forest; **Mike Feddersen**, Diablo 4 Wheelers, for his help with the Bear Valley OHV Loop Trail; and **Clarence Solari** for a great ride on Sierra Trek. They aided in presenting complete and accurate information.

Special thanks go to **Cory Fitzpatrick** for her skillful editing and **Anne Holms** for her excellent proofreading.

For those who wonder…how did you do that…here is the technical information. The Guide was written on a PC using Microsoft Word 2000 and published with PageMaker 6.52. The graphics were prepared using the "all powerful" Photoshop 6.0. The pictures and artwork were scanned using an HP ScanJet IIcx.

History of the Tahoe National Forest

The Tahoe National Forest has been referred to as a "history rich" environment. The area is in the heart of the Sierra Nevada which contain important geological history. The Native Americans lived in the area for thousands of years before the immigrants moved from the east, discovered gold, and built railroads and highways.

Geology

The Tahoe National Forest straddles the Sierra Nevada Mountains from the foothills near Grass Valley and Nevada City to the foothills just west of Reno. This area encompasses some of the most interesting geology in the United States.

There were many phases in the development of the present day Sierra Nevada. Millions of years ago, the area was dominated by what is called the Ancestral Yuba River (Figure 1). This river generally flowed north to south. It cut through gold-bearing mountains that existed then, and in the process, the gold was mixed with the gravels. In time, volcanic activity covered part of the area with lava flows.

Then about 3 million years ago, as volcanic activity lessened, there was a rapid tilting of the Sierra block, which became the Sierra Nevada. As a result, the drainage flow was now from east to west. Over time the rivers we call the Feather, Yuba, and American cut deep chan-

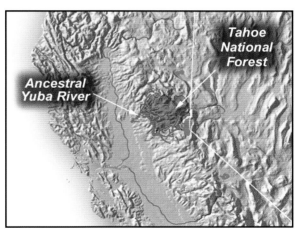

Figure 1. *The gravels of the Ancestral Yuba River was the source of much of the gold recovered during the California gold rush.*

nels into the gravels of the Ancestral Yuba River, exposing the rich gold-laden river bed. Layers of these gravel deposits were known as the "Great Blue Lead," named for their bluish color (Figure 2).

Another feature of the Sierra Nevada are its many lakes, most of which are the result of glacial action. As glaciers moved through the area, they gouged out holes in the granite rock which formed lakes and meadows. Another sign of glacial activity is the many light-colored granite boulders, or "erratics," dotting the landscape. These boulders were picked up by a moving glacier and dropped as it receded, leaving them in some unusual places.

Native American Use

The Nisenan people, a subgroup of the Maidu, lived in the area thousands of years before the white man invaded their lands (Figure 3). Their permanent homes were in the foothills, where the snow wasn't too deep in the winter months. They were a very territorial people. They moved high up into the Sierra in the spring to hunt, fish and gather roots, berries and other foodstuffs.

The Native American people of the Sierra Nevada traded goods on an west-to-east pattern. They used the "fine-grained" basalt for tools and arrowheads. There was very little contact with tribes north or south of their territories and trading routes. In some cases, tribes could not speak with people a few miles north or south of them because of the differences in the languages.

Figure 2. The "Great Blue Lead" marked the location of the historic Ancestral Yuba River. This gold-rich gravel was the source of millions of dollars worth in of gold. This outcropping is just north of the Forest City Museum.

The Sierra was rich with plant and animal life. The land and those that inhabited it were in balance. The Native Americans had the greatest respect for nature and what it provided them. This changed as Europeans began to explore the area and inhabit the land.

The Nisenan culture goes back about 4,000 years. They were a very well organized culture and numbered in the tens of thousands until the Spanish moved into the missions and the trading "networks" carried the European diseases with them. Close to 75 percent of the native population was killed by small pox and other "white man's" diseases. The emigrants refer to the Native America Tribes (of California) as small bands of meek people – their numbers and community organizations had been decimated. One interesting difference between the mountain people and those that lived in the valleys was that the mountain people cremated their dead, where as the valley people buried their dead.

If you know what to look for, you can often find things they left behind, such as grinding holes in rock outcroppings, stone chips where they made arrowheads or other rock tools, or petroglyph art. **Warning**: If you do find signs of Native American activity, please leave it as you found it…besides being the right thing to do, it is the Law!

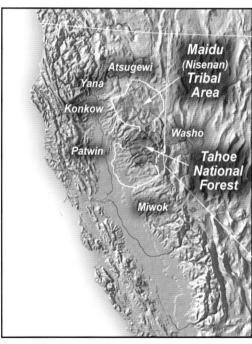

Figure 3. The Nisenan people lived in what is now known as the Tahoe National Forest.

Although the Spanish (1768 to 1822) and the Mexicans (1822 to 1846), had explored and settled in California, there is no record that they ventured very far into Tahoe National Forest. John C. Fremont's third expedition crossed the Sierra at Donner Summit a couple of weeks ahead of the Stephens-Townsend-Murphy Party. They arrived at Sutter's Fort on December 9, 1844.

Stephens-Townsend-Murphy Party

The first thing you think of when studying Emigrant Trails is Donner Summit and the Donner Party. But the first wagon trains to use it were in the Stephens-Townsend-Murphy Party from Council Bluffs, Iowa. This 50-person party crossed the Sierra, on the "Truckee Route," in November 1844.

In the spring of 1844, hundreds of emigrants were "staged" in Southwestern Iowa, wanting to head west and toward "their destiny." Most of the emigrants were heading to Oregon, but this small band, made up of ten families, started their journey to California on May 22, 1844 (Figure 4).

Figure 4. The Oregon-California Trail took the emigrants west after crossing the Missouri River. The Stephens-Townsend-Murphy Party went north, through Fort Hall, Idaho. The Donner Party thought they were taking a shortcut by taking the Hastings Cutoff.

The group was diverse, Stephens was a blacksmith and captain in the U.S. Army (resigned), Townsend was a doctor, and Murphy was a farmer. The mighty Missouri River, the first of 18 rivers they would cross, was their first obstacle. The party followed the well-marked wagon trail westward. By July they were in Wyoming, crossing the Rocky Mountains through South Pass. From Fort Bridger they took what was called the Greenwood Cutoff toward Fort Hall, Idaho. They left Fort Hall on August 15, moving southwest into Nevada, where they followed the Humboldt River.

Moving west they crossed the Nevada desert until they reached what today is the Reno area and the Truckee River. The Truckee River was named for Chief Truckee, the chief of the

Paiute Indian Nation. The emigrants assumed that the Chief's name was Truckee, because he used the word so often. In actuality, the word "truk-ee" is Paiute for "all right" or "very well."

The party slowly moved up the Truckee River, crossing back and forth several times in each mile they traveled. On November 14th they arrived where Donner Creek meets the Truckee River. The next day the party split up, with four men and two women on horseback, following the main river south to its origin, Lake Tahoe — then up McKinney Creek and down the Rubicon and American Rivers to Sacramento. They arrived on December 10, 1844. These six people were the first "white men" to view Lake Tahoe.

The rest of the party followed Donner Creek west to Donner Lake where it was beginning to snow. It took them ten days to move five wagons over the summit. They left six wagons and three young men to guard them near Donner Lake. The party had to build a "survival camp" near what is now Big Bend. A rescue party left Big Bend on December 6th for Sacramento; they arrived on December 13th. Before they could return to Big Bend, John Sutter enlisted them to help him fight what was called the "Micheltorena War." This battle lasted for about a month. The rescue party left Sacramento on February 20, 1845 to bring the rest of the party out of the mountains. By early March 1845, all of the party, plus two children born on the trip, arrived at Fort Sutter in Sacramento.

This proved that wagons could be taken through the Sierra Nevada to California. More were to follow. In 1846, close to 400 wagons were moved along the Truckee Trail before the ill-fated Donner Party attemped to pass through the mountains.

Donner-Reed Party

The Donner-Reed Party was a "hodge-podge" of 87 individuals from Illinois, Iowa, Tennessee, Missouri, and Ohio. In May 1846, the party crossed the Missouri River and began following the Platte River west. On July 4th, they were in Fort Laramie. On July 30, the party left Fort Bridger and the Oregon Trail, taking the newly established Hastings Cutoff. They had been convinced that this was a shorter route. By the end of August they were at the south end of the Great Salt Lake. The Hastings Cutoff proved to be "technically" shorter, but the route was very difficult, and added a full month to their journey.

By October 20th the Donner-Reed Party was on the Truckee River west of Reno. As the party moved west, they left the Truckee River at Verdi. (Note: The Stephens-Townsend-Murphy Party was the last group to follow the Truckee River. Members of the Stephens Party established the new route that the Donner-Reed Party used during the summer of 1847.) This was an easier route that eventually became part of the Henness Pass Road and the Lincoln Highway.

The story of the Donner-Reed Party is one of poor leadership, bad decisions and an early winter. An advance party of four men, including James Reed, reached Sutter's Fort about the same time the rest of the party with the wagons, reached Donner Lake. There were two campsites where the party "holed up" for the winter. The Donner Family stopped about seven miles short of the Donner Lake site. This site is now used as a Forest Service Picnic Area. The main campsite for the party was located on the east end of Donner Lake, now the site of a memorial and Emigrant Trail Museum.

The history of the trip from the crossing of the Missouri River to Sutter's Fort is one of misery. Before the party reached Donner Lake, several had died along the way. There was even a stabbing in self-defense in which James Reed killed John Snyder.

The first big storm occurred October 28 and lasted about two weeks. Once the storm subsided, the first attempt to cross the summit was made. This attempt and one a week later failed. About December 15th, two more storms had hit the area and the first emigrant died of starvation. Additional storms hit the area on December 23, January 9 and 22, February 2, March 6 and 28.

From Sutter's Fort, James Reed was working hard to gather relief supplies. On November 4 the first rescue attempt was made. They were stopped by deep snow and had to return to Sutter's Fort. Over the next several months several attempts were made to rescue the party and the party made several attempts to escape. However, not all of the deaths occurred east of the summit. Some died west of the summit at the "Camp of Death" located near what is now called Emigrant Gap. A total of 42 individuals died, two of them were rescuers; only 49 of the original party reached California.

(Note: If you want more information regarding the Donner-Reed Party, read C. F. McGlashan's *History of the Donner Party, a Tragedy of the Sierra.*)

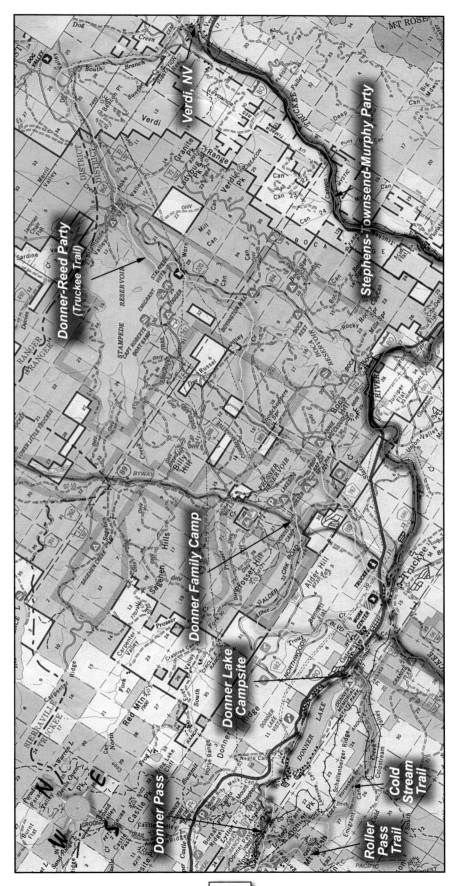

Donner-Reed Party
(Truckee Trail)

Verdi, NV

Stephens-Townsend-Murphy Party

Donner Family Camp

Donner Lake Campsite

Donner Pass

Cold Stream Trail

Roller Pass Trail

Gold Mining

The discovery of gold in 1848 forever changed California. The miners brought their diseases, culture and laws, and the desire for riches brought more miners.

There were several phases to gold mining in California. The first phase involved working the rivers and streams with pans, sluices, and rocker boxes. Once "49ers" discovered there were rich gravel deposits, they devised methods to extract it in large operations. Some of these deposits were found under the lava flow posed some special problems. (Note: The major lava flows, volcanic or mud, on the Tahoe National Forest all have their origins from Mt. Rose, located just seven miles north of Lake Tahoe. This flow extended all the way to what is now Douglas Boulevard in Placer County.)

The second phase of gold mining used hydraulic mining methods. From 1853 to 1856, hydraulic mining evolved from the use of hoses to wash moderate amounts of water over the gold-baring gravels, to the use of large nozzles or "monitors." Hydraulicking was widespread. The largest operation, the Malakoff Diggings eight miles northeast of Nevada City, used up to 60 million gallons of water a day to wash 50,000 tons of soil down through a drain tunnel. So much debris clogged the South Yuba and Sacramento Rivers that in 1884, Federal Judge Lorenzo Sawyer stopped the operation as a result of a lawsuit (See page 137 for more detailed information).

Drift mining was also used to get to the gold. The miners would find gravel deposits and just follow them where ever they went under ground. From time-to-time, they would find pockets of gold nuggets worth millions of dollars.

There were several hard-rock mines on the Forest. In Alleghany, the gold-bearing (quartz) ore was exposed on the surface. Later, tunnels were dug down to quartz-bearing rock that was then brought to the surface, reduced to gravel in a stamp mill, and mercury was used to extract the gold from the slurry. The Sixteen-to-One Mine in Allegany was the last of these type mines to operate on the Forest.

Transcontinental Railroad

The building of the transcontinental railroad was one of the most notable feats of its time. Several factors played part in this venture. There was the desire of President Lincoln to tie this

Nation together during the Civil War. There was the desire of four entrepreneurs in California (namely Leland Stanford, C. P. Huntington, Charles Crocker, and Mark Hopkins) to move commerce from Coast-to-Coast. There were the incentives provided by the Federal Government, and there was the availability of thousands of laborers, namely the Chinese.

Ever since gold was discovered in the new state of California, there was a desire to tie the extensive railroad systems of the east with the Pacific Ocean. Many routes were proposed, but the one that went from Omaha, Nebraska to Sacramento was specified in the Pacific Railroad Act of 1862.

The plan was to start building from both ends. The Union Pacific would start in Omaha and move west on a route engineered by Grenville Dodge. The Central Pacific Railroad would start from Sacramento and head east on a route engineered by Theodore Judah. Even though they had a route and authorization, the two companies needed about $100 million to build it! (That was more than twice the total federal budget.) In 1863, construction began, but was very slow because of the lack of funds. In the first year, the Union Pacific laid only 40 miles of track and the Central Pacific only 20 miles.

Several funding sources were used. The four entrepreneurs put up their own cash and the state of California pledged $10,000 for every mile of track laid. The Federal Acts of 1862 and 1864 authorized the payment of $16,000 per mile of track on level ground and $48,000 per mile for track in mountainous country, plus the ownership of every other section of land for ten miles on each side of the tracks. In addition, there were millions of dollars of stocks sold.

At one time there were over 10,000 laborers working on the construction of the railroad through the Sierra Nevada, each being paid $1 a day. By July 1866 the line reached Dutch Flat. By the fall, the line had reached Cisco. In the spring of 1868, it reached the Summit tunnel east of Cisco. Since the roadway was constructed in sections, once the tunnel was completed, the rails were laid quickly.

By June 1868, the first run from Sacramento into the Nevada Territory and Lake's Station (Reno), was made. On April 28, 1869, 10 miles and 56 feet of track was laid in a twelve-hour shift. On May 10, 1869, the tracks joined at Promontory Point, Utah. It is interesting to note that on this monumental day, both Leland Sanford (President of Central Pacific Railroad) and Thomas Durant

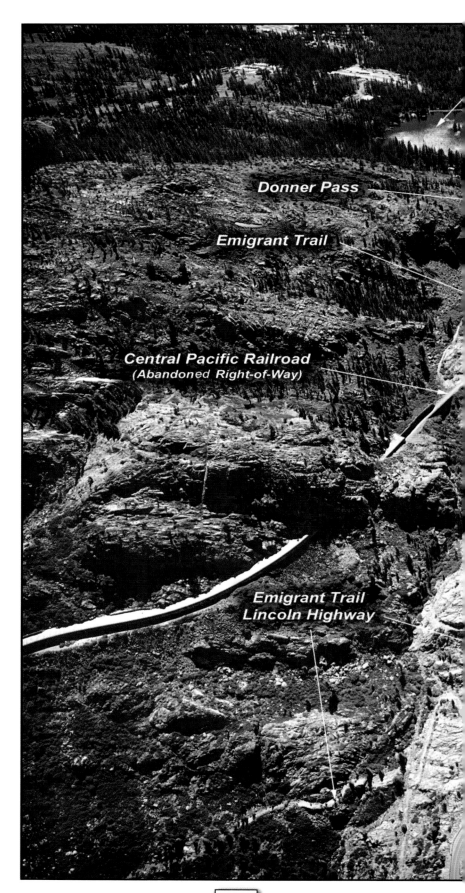

Donner Pass

Emigrant Trail

Central Pacific Railroad
(Abandoned Right-of-Way)

Emigrant Trail
Lincoln Highway

Donner Ski Ranch

ry

Rainbow Bridge

Old U.S. Highway 40

(President of the Union Pacific Railroad) missed hitting the golden spike on their first attempts. Once the railroad was completed, it cut travel from Omaha to San Francisco from months to days. It truly tied this great Nation together.

However, this did not mark the end of railroading on the Tahoe National Forest. Between 1868 and 1930 there were standard and narrow-gauge railroad tracks laid all through the area of the Forest north of Interstate 80, west to Webber Lake, north to Loyalton, and east to Dog Valley. There were logging spurs that tied with the Central Pacific line at Boca and went up the Little Truckee River through Sardine Valley and down Smithneck Creek to Loyalton. Another spur went northwest from Sardine Valley up through the Bear Valley Trail area to within a couple of miles of Sierraville. There was another standard gauge spur that went from Truckee north to Hobart Mill following what is now Highway 89.

Logging Activities

As the population grew so did the need for lumber. Heavy timbers, lumber and other wood products were in great demand by the railroad and the mining industry in both California and Nevada. The timber resources that are now within Tahoe National Forest were the main source. Remember, the railroad owned every other section of land, for ten miles on each side of the tracks. Also, in those early days there was little enforcement of timber trespass on federal land.

The railroad was the main form of transportation for logs and lumber. On the larger lakes, such as Lake Tahoe, the logs were formed into rafts and moved to the mills. Most of the timber that is seen today on the Forest, is second or third generation, or crop since these forests were first logged over a hundred years ago. In 1890 there were 21 large sawmills on the forest between Downieville and Truckee.

Tahoe National Forest

The Forest Reserve Act of 1891 established the National Forest System. Even though the law allowed the President to set aside lands as forest reserves established in 1881, it wasn't until 1899 when President McKinley established the 136 thousand acre Lake Tahoe Forest Reserve. In 1905, President Roosevelt expanded the Tahoe Reserve and a year later established the 800,000 acres, Tahoe National Forest.

The Tahoe National Forest was not only a producer of timber and gold, it was also a source of water for domestic and agricultural purposes, water for hydroelectric power generation, and the land was used to graze cattle and sheep. People from the San Francisco Bay area and the Central Valley, as well as the Nevada mining districts also used the Forest for recreation.

Lincoln Highway

In the first decade of the 20th century, most of the roads in the United States were dirt and if you were lucky, level and graveled. Also, most of the roads did not really lead anywhere. In 1912, Carl Fisher, owner of the Indianapolis Motor Speedway proposed "Coast-to-Coast Rock Highway," and to have the graveled highway completed by the time the 1915 Panama-Pacific Exposition opened in San Francisco.

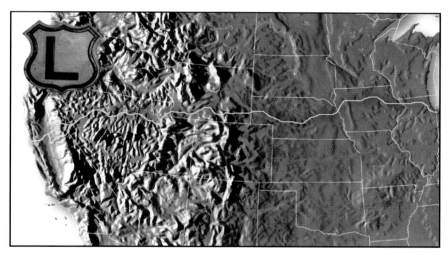

Figure 5. The Lincoln Highway was the first coast-to-coast highway in the United States.

The Lincoln Highway (Figure 5) was proposed in July 1913 as a transcontinental route, linking the Atlantic and Pacific Oceans together. The plan was to utilize existing roads and new construction to have a highway from New York City, via Chicago, Salt Lake City, Reno, Sacramento, and ending in San Francisco. The route was eventually marked with concrete markers placed by the Boy Scouts of America. A marker, like the one to the right, can be seen about 500-feet east (downhill) of the Rainbow Bridge overlook.

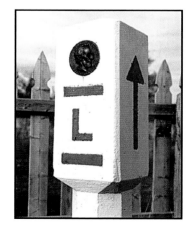

In 1927 the Lincoln Highway was designated US 40. It was the main highway across the Sierra Nevada until Interstate 80 was opened in 1964.

Figure 6. This is said to be the most beautiful bridge on the Lincoln Highway. In actuality, the Rainbow Bridge was constructed when the highway was designated U.S. Highway 40.

Forest Service
Rules and Regulations

The USDA Forest Service manages most of the land over which you will be traveling. This section of the Guide outlines the applicable rules and regulations pertaining to the use of the Forest. For more information, visit their homepage at:

http://www.r5.fs.fed.us/tahoe/

Hunting

Hunting is permitted in most of the forest at certain times of the year. Popular game animals are deer and quail. All hunting on private and federally owned land is regulated by the California Department of Fish and Game, and a license is required. Any animal not listed as a game animal in the California hunting regulations is protected, therefore, cannot be hunted.

Keep in mind you can't just go out in the woods and take target practice. Be sure to check with the Forest Service on where and when you can target shoot.

Fishing

Public lakes and streams in the forest are regularly stocked with trout in the spring and summer. A state license is required in order to fish.

Camping

Camping areas, developed by the Forest Service, are numerous and are open from May to October. Most campsites are on a first-come, first-serve basis, but there are special sites that can be reserved. It is advisable to make reservations 7 to 10 days in advance. There usually is a nominal fee. Call the Forest Service to make reservations. There are three types of camping areas:

- Family campgrounds are generally equipped with vault or flush toilets, fire rings and/or stoves, tables and parking spaces. Fees are charged and drinking water is available.

- Group campgrounds can accommodate 10 to 100 people; reservations are required.

- Undeveloped camping includes all the varieties of camping outside of a developed site.

Generally you can camp anywhere on lands managed by the USDA Forest Service and the Bureau of Land Management. But in the Lakes Basin Recreation Area, you can only camp in designated campgrounds. If you camp in a designated campground, you do not need a Campfire Permit. If you plan on camping elsewhere, you **will need a permit**, even if you will be using a camp stove.

Green Sticker Vehicles

All Green Sticker vehicles are off-highway vehicles, but not all off-highway vehicles are Green Sticker vehicles. A Green Sticker vehicle is a legal non-street legal vehicle (cannot be operated on city streets, county roads or state highways) that can be licensed to operate on designated dirt roads and trails. These vehicles include three and four wheel all-terrain vehicles (ATV) and cross-country motorcycles (dirt bikes). Green Sticker vehicles get their name from the color of the sticker provided by the Department of Motor Vehicles indicating they have been properly registered.

Green Sticker vehicles can use some of the trails described in this guide. There are also many other Green Sticker vehicle trails— contact the Forest Service or Bureau of Land Management for details.

There are some special requirements that must be met before you can operate a Green Sticker vehicle:

- All vehicles not registered for highway use are required to have a "green sticker" affixed to the vehicle in the designated location for that vehicle.

- All vehicles are required to have a properly installed and operating USDA Forest Service approved spark arrester and muffler.

- All Green Sticker vehicles and dual sport motorcycles are required to meet State sound regulations (less than 101 decibels).

- Registration: All riders are required to carry proof of ownership while operating any motorized vehicle on public lands.

- State law requires that you slow your vehicle down to 15 miles-per-hour when passing within 50 feet of another person, vehicle, or livestock.

- The operator must wear a safety helmet meeting standards adopted by the US Department of Transportation.

- It is illegal to carry a passenger on an ATV.

- All riders under the age of 18 are required to have a State ATV Safety Certificate of Completion in order to operate an ATV, or be under the direct supervision of an adult who has proof of completing the safety course.

- Direct supervision by a parent or guardian is required for all riders of ATV's under the age of 14, in addition to the above safety requirements.

- All "driving under influence" laws apply to OHV operations.

Winter Access

Most of the higher elevation roads are closed to "wheeled" vehicle traffic during the winter, but open for snowmobiles. Be sure to check with the Forest Service before you venture too far and that you are prepared if you become snowbound.

Pets

All pets must be kept on a leash in campgrounds, picnic areas, and on the trail. This will help protect your dog from having an encounter with a skunk, porcupine, or be found by a hungry cougar.

Archeological Sites

Laws protects archeological sites. A site can be defined by a single arrowhead or bedrock mortar. Leave things you find as they are.

Pacific Crest National Scenic Trail

As you travel though the Tahoe National Forest, you will cross paths with the Pacific Crest National Scenic Trail. This trail extends 2,650 miles from Mexico to Canada. It is intended for the use of hikers and horses, not for motor vehicles or bicycles, and you will be cited if you violate this rule. If you want more information about this famous trail, contact the Pacific Crest Trail Association at *www.pcta.org*

Trip Logistics

Being stranded in the middle of the Tahoe National Forest is not the place to be when you remember you forgot a very important item(s). This section of the Guide has been developed to help you plan for and carry the important things you will need on an overnight trip on one of the many trails. One good thing about visiting the Tahoe National Forest is that you are never very far from stores or lodging.

MOST IMPORTANT ITEMS

❏ A *four-wheel drive rig* that is equipped to handle the magnitude of challenges you are planning to attempt.

❏ A *group* of other four-wheelers who will travel with you.

❏ *4 Wheeler's Guide - Trails of the Tahoe National Forest.*

Personal Items

❏ Sleeping Bag
❏ Cot or Bed Pad
❏ Tent or Tarp
❏ Personal items
❏ Prescriptions
❏ Flashlight and Batteries
❏ Towel
❏ Toilet Paper
❏ Aspirin, etc.
❏ Camera and film
❏ Extra set of clothing
❏ Jacket
❏ Rain Gear
❏ Gloves
❏ Insect Repellent
❏ Extra Eyeglasses
❏ Extra Car Keys
❏ First Aid Kit
❏ Trash Bag(s)
❏ _____
❏ _____

Camping Items

- ❏ Campfire Permit
- ❏ Stove
- ❏ Lantern and Fuel
- ❏ Pots and Pans
- ❏ Matches
- ❏ Garbage Bags
- ❏ Dishes/utensils, etc.
- ❏ Food and Drink
- ❏ Water
- ❏ Shovel and Axe
- ❏ _____
- ❏ _____

Equipment-related Items

- ❏ Tools
- ❏ Fire Extinguisher
- ❏ Fuses
- ❏ Heavy-duty jack
- ❏ CB Radio
- ❏ Jumper Cables
- ❏ _____

Equipment within the Group

- ❏ Tow Straps
- ❏ Extra Axles
- ❏ Motor Oil
- ❏ Brake Fluid
- ❏ Transmission Fluid
- ❏ Gear oil and Bearing Grease
- ❏ Come-a-long
- ❏ Duct and Electrical Tape
- ❏ Snatch Block
- ❏ Cell Phone
- ❏ Kitty Litter or other absorbant
- ❏ _____
- ❏ _____
- ❏ _____
- ❏ _____
- ❏ _____
- ❏ _____
- ❏ _____
- ❏ _____

Trail Etiquette and Safety

When driving the trails of the Tahoe National Forest, special "rules of the road" should be followed. You will be traveling through one of the most magnificent areas in the Sierra Nevada's are expected to leave only footprints or tire tracks. You will also be using trails that in some places are barely wide enough for your vehicle, let alone two vehicles.

This section of the Guide outlines some specific rules that should be followed while on the trail. Most of them are common sense, but several of them apply specifically to all back country driving.

As a visitor to private lands and National Forest System lands, you are expected to treat the land with respect and care. The only indication that you have visited the area should be your footprints and tire tracks. Trash, cans and other refuse should be packaged and taken home for disposal. Adopt the attitude that you want to leave the area at least as clean as you found it.

Tread Lightly! ®

Tread Lightly!, Inc. is a nonprofit corporation that seeks to educate the outdoor recreationist, as well as the media and suppliers of outdoor related materials, on ways to treat the outdoors in a responsible manner. There are five basic principles in the Tread Lightly! Program Pledge:

> Travel only where permitted
> Respect the rights of others
> Educate yourself
> Avoid streams, meadows, wildlife areas, etc.
> Drive and travel responsibly

To achieve these principles you will have to be properly prepared, use common sense, be courteous, and respect the environment.

Tread Lightly! also means "Leaving No Trace" of your visit. To accomplish this you should:

- *Plan ahead - Be properly prepared, and have the right equipment. Know where you are going and what you will need to make the trip enjoyable.*

- *Camp at existing and legal campsites - don't just camp anywhere.*
- *Travel on existing, durable surfaces - don't travel off the established path. Only travel across surfaces that will safely support your vehicle and will not show that you have been there.*
- *Pack it in...pack it out! Leave only your tracks.*
- *Properly dispose of what you cannot pack out. Be sure that if you have to leave something behind, it will not be easily found by those who follow or by bears.*
- *Leave what you find. If you pick up that rock or pluck that flower, it will not be there for the next visitor. Pictures are the only things you should take.*
- *Minimize the use of fire. A wildfire can change an area for hundreds of years. Use fire wisely and safely.*

Note: For more information regarding minimum impact four wheeling, contact Tread Lightly!, Inc. Their address and telephone number can be found in the appendix.

Rules of the Road

One thing you will not find on the trail is a white line, so, normal DMV traffic rules will not be enough. These are some of the more important rules of the road:

- *Stay on the trail or roadway. Don't drive through "untracked" terrain trying to be the first ever to drive your four-wheeler "where no man has gone before." Don't make your own shortcut or trail.*
- *If you go through a gate, leave it as you found it. Nothing makes a landowner more upset than when a gate's position is changed, cutting off livestock from food or water, or allowing them to escape.*
- *If you are about to enter private land, be sure you get permission first.*
- *Keep the noise and dust down. Both are a form of "pollution" and you should respect others who are on the trail with you.*
- *Yield the right of way to bikers, hikers and people on horseback. Be especially careful around animals. Pull to the side of the road; turn off your engine and be still and quiet until they pass.*
- *Yield the right-of-way to drivers on the uphill grade or those who are overtaking you.*
- *Take a track down the middle of the trail if you can. Avoid widening the trail.*

- *Cross streams only at fording points.*
- *Avoid unnessary wheel spinning.*

Safety on the Road

Nothing will spoil a trip quicker than if someone gets hurt or a rig becomes seriously damaged. The key to a safe trip is respect for the trail and knowing the limitations of your skills, and the capabilities of your rig. You should follow these "common sense" safety rules:

- *Buckle up! This isn't a suggestion...it is mandatory that everyone be properly secured in the rig.*
- *Travel with a group and preferably with someone who has been on the trail before.*
- *Have a citizen's band radio. Establish the "tactical net" you will be using as a group. Having a cellular phone can also be helpful.*
- *Don't drink and drive. The correlation between drinking alcohol and damage or injury is significant. Besides, it's against the law.*
- *Build plenty of time into your schedule so that you don't have to drive after dark.*
- *Keep a reasonable distance between rigs. Give those around you plenty of room to maneuver.*
- *Do not speed or use the trail for racing.*

Trail Difficulty Ratings

Several trail difficulty rating systems have been developed. The Forest Service has developed a system that uses three adjectives, "easiest," "more difficult," and "most difficult." Jeepers Jamboree, USA, uses a scale from one to ten, with the Rubicon Trail being given a rating of 10. The Red Rock 4-Wheelers of Utah has developed a four-point scale to define the difficulty on the trails of Moab. In this section of the Guide, an attempt will be made to compare each of these trail difficulty ratings against the Forest Service system, the one being used in this Guide.

Four-Wheel Drive "Difficulty" Guide

	Easiest	More Difficult	Most Difficult
Grade			
Maximum Sustained (200 - 300 feet)	20%	20%	30%
Maximum Pitch	20%	30%	50%
Clearance			
Width	Ample clearance for logging trucks.	12.5 feet	8 feet
Height		9 feet	8 feet
Travel Way			
Width	10 feet	5.0' for 70" vehicle width. (hub-to-hub)	
Surface	Rough, irregular. Travel with low-clearance vehicles is difficult.	Some sections are relatively rough. Large rocks, mud holes, loose material. Might require some winching.	Rough to very rough. Long sections of loose rock, sand, mud. Stream crossings and large boulders. Winching sections.

Source: USDA Forest Service Trails Management Handbook

Easiest

The easiest trails don't normally need four-wheel drive vehicles, but clearance may be a problem for some vehicles. This rating includes all-weather roads or roads that may need four-wheel vehicles when the weather is poor. These trails get a Jeepers Jamboree rating of 1 to 2 and a Moab rating of 1 to 2.

More Difficult

The more difficult trails are just that, a little more difficult. Four-wheel drive will be required because the trail will be steep, muddy, and rocky, and may be "loose." There may even be a need to winch or assist others with a tow. The driver will need to know the capability of his or her vehicle and will need to know something about four-wheel driving. These trails get a Jeepers Jamboree rating of 3 to 6 and a Moab rating of 2½ to 3.

Most Difficult

The most difficult trails are ones that will really test the capabilities of the vehicle and driver. Although most trails are not rated as "most difficult" for the full length of the trail, certain sections challenge to this level. For a trail to get this rating, the terrain must be so tough that specially equipped vehicles are recommended AND the driver should be experienced. On a "most difficult" section of trail, you may encounter badly eroded ruts, large boulders, steep drops/climbs and conditions you may not even want to walk through. On the more challenging trails, you should expect some damage to vehicles. These trails get a Jeepers Jamboree rating of 7 to 9 and a Moab rating of 3½ to 4+.

General Area Maps

In this section of the Guide you will find a series of maps that cover the Tahoe National Forest north of Interstate 80. The base map used on the next several pages, is the 1995 edition of the USDA Forest Service map for the Tahoe National Forest. The scale of these maps is roughly $5/8$-inch equals 1 mile. Forest Service recreational sites are indicated in red.

The "green lands" are managed and protected by the Forest Service; the "salmon lands" are managed by the Bureau of Land Management and the "white lands" are privately owned.

Each of the trails presented in this Guide are highlighted in yellow. Other trails are highlighted in blue. These are other OHV trails you may want to explore.

Use the following maps to get to and from the specific trails. Use the topographic maps for more detail.

Note: If you would like a copy of the Tahoe National Forest map, contact the Forest Service at any of the offices listed in the appendix. There will be a nominal fee.

Legend

————	National Forest Boundary
— —— —	Adjacent National Forest Boundary
— — — —	State Boundary
— — —	County Boundary
▪ — — ▪	Ranger District Boundary
▒▒▒▒	Special Area Boundary
5	Primary Forest Route
10N44	Forest Route
————	Primary Highway
———	Secondary Highway
———	Improved Road, Paved
▪—▪—▪	Improved Road, Gravel
———	Improved Road, Dirt
- - - - - -	Unimproved Road
_ _ OHV _ _	Off Highway Vehicle Road
- - - - - -	Trail
_ _ OHV	Off Highway Vehicle Trail

Forest Supervisor Office
Ranger Office — Report Fires Here
Other Forest Service Facility
Campground — Forest Service Recreation Sites
Group Campground
Undeveloped Campsite
Picnic Area, Day Use Only
Visitor Information Center
Trailhead
Campground other than Forest Service
Picnic Area other than Forest Service
Pack Station
Scenic Viewpoint
Wildlife Viewing Area
Public Telephone
Resort
Boat Launching Ramp
Ski Area
Sno-Park
Avalanche Control Area
Permanent Lookout Station
Spring
Located or Landmark Object
House, Cabin or other Building
School, Church
Sawmill
Heliport
Trailer Sanitary Station
Locked Gate, All Year Closure
Locked Gate, Seasonal Closure
Mine
National Scenic Byway
National Forest
Adjacent National Forest
National Forest Wilderness
State Land
BLM Land

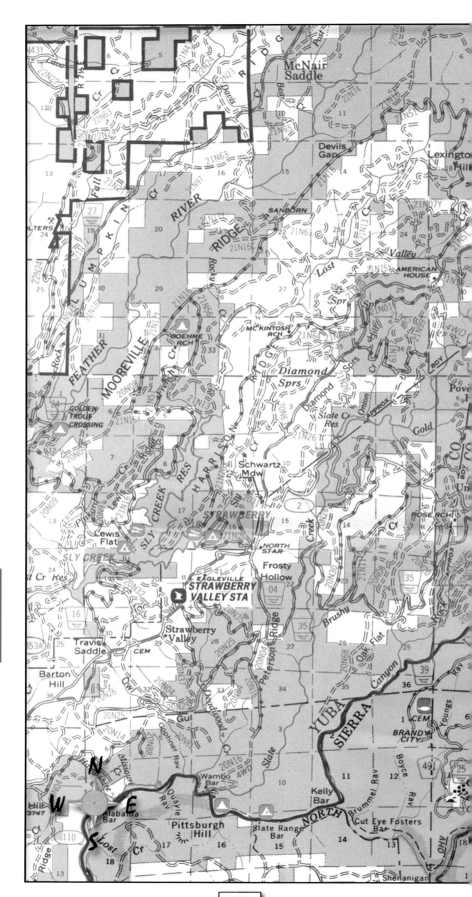

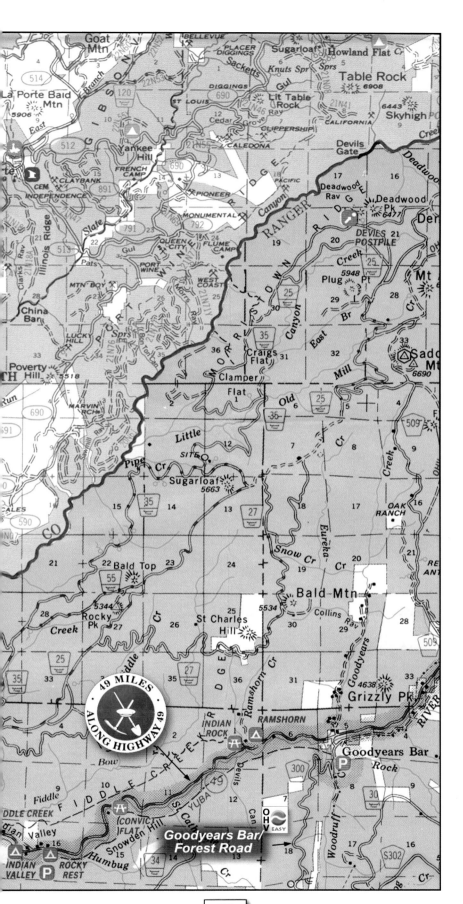

Poker Flat Trail

Chimney Rock Trail

Craycroft Ridge Trail

Downie River Trail

Fir Cap Trail

49 MILES ALONG HIGHWAY 49

Goodyears Bar/ Forest Road

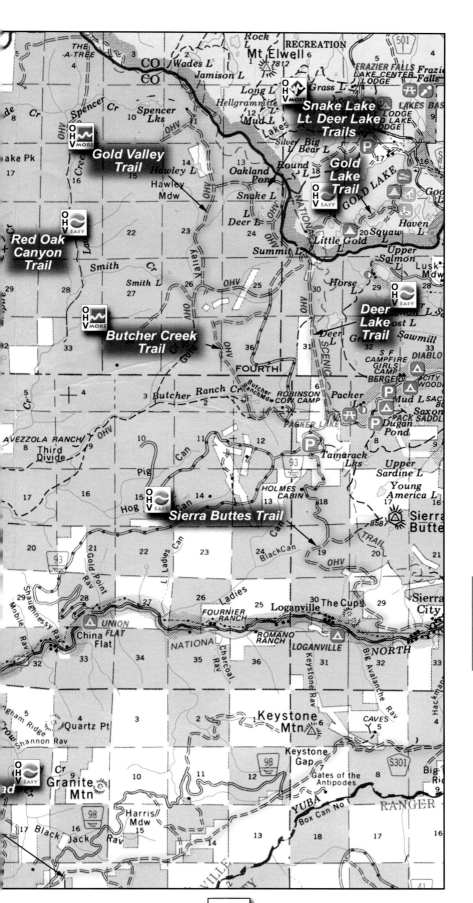

Gold Valley
Trail

Red Oak
Canyon
Trail

Butcher Creek
Trail

Sierra Buttes Trail

Snake Lake
Lt. Deer Lake
Trails

Gold
Lake
Trail

Deer
Lake
Trail

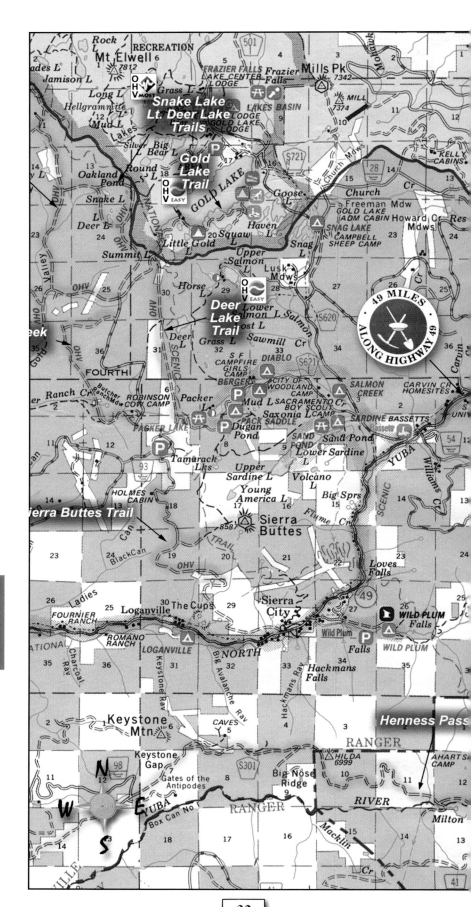

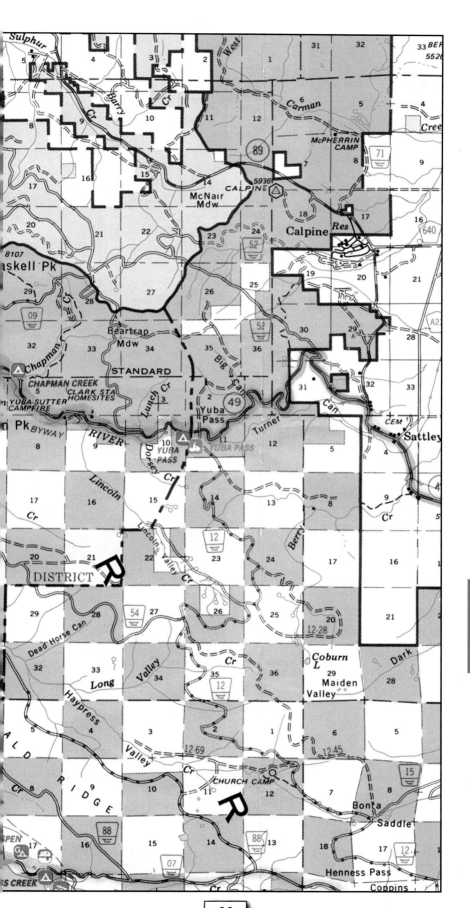

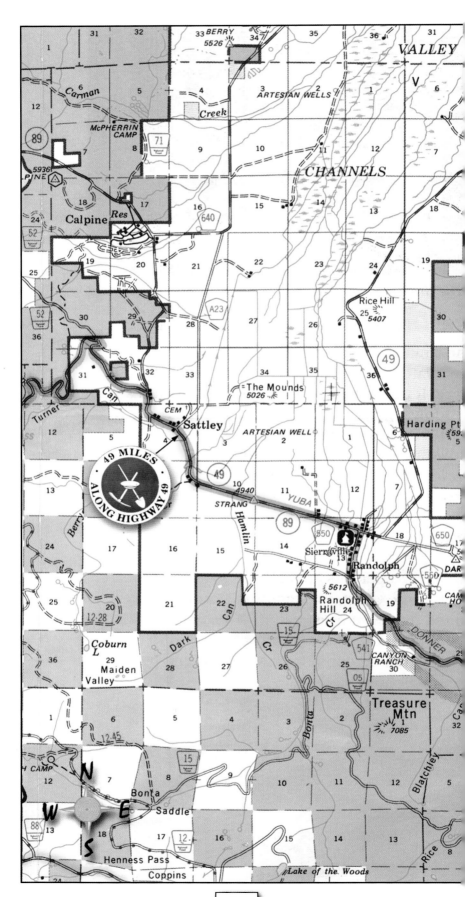

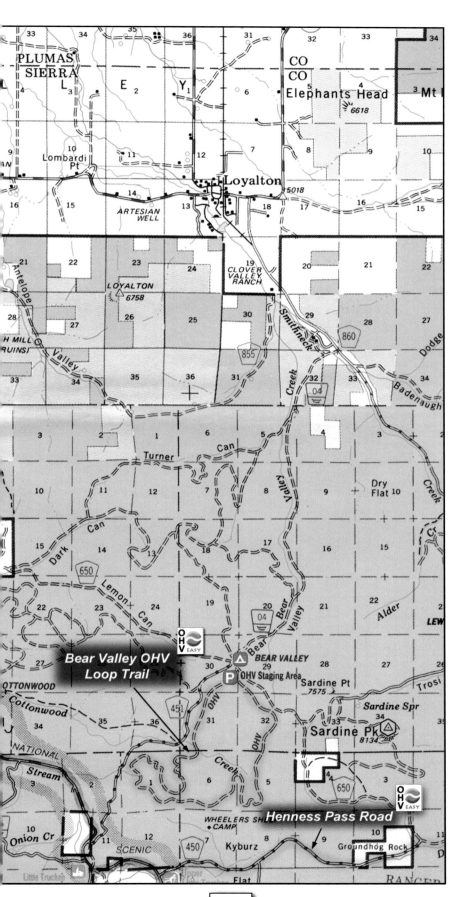

PLUMAS
SIERRA

Loyalton

Elephants Head
6618

Lombardi
Pt

ARTESIAN
WELL

5018

CLOVER
VALLEY
RANCH

LOYALTON
6758

Smithneck

860

855

Creek

04

Dodge

Valley

Badenaugh

H MILL
RUINS)

Antelope

Turner   Can

Dry
Flat

Creek

Valley

Dark   Can

650

Cr

Lemon   Can

04

Bear   Valley

Alder

LEW

**Bear Valley OHV
Loop Trail**

OHV EASY

Bear

BEAR VALLEY
OHV Staging Area

OTTONWOOD

P

Sardine Pt
7575

Trosi

Cottonwood

451

OHV

Sardine Spr

NATIONAL

Creek

Sardine Pk
8134

Stream

650

OHV EASY

Onion Cr

WHEELERS SH
CAMP

Henness Pass Road

Groundhog Rock

SCENIC

450

Kyburz

Little Truckee

Flat

RANGER

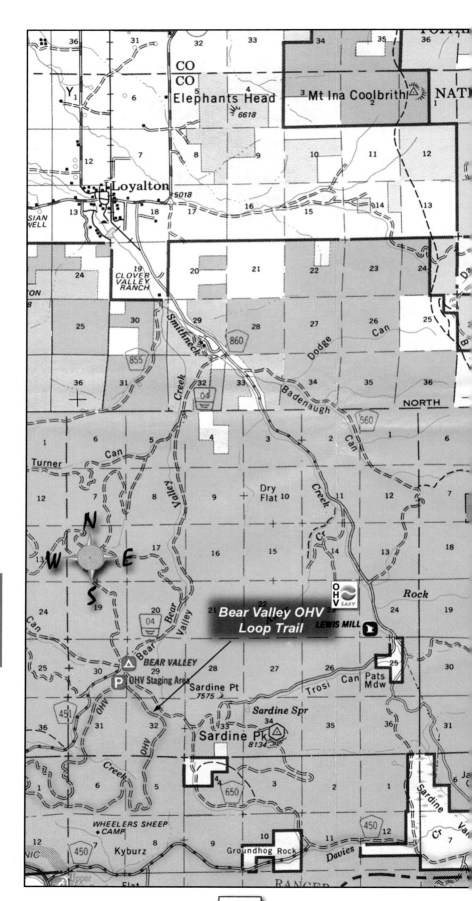

Bear Valley OHV Loop Trail

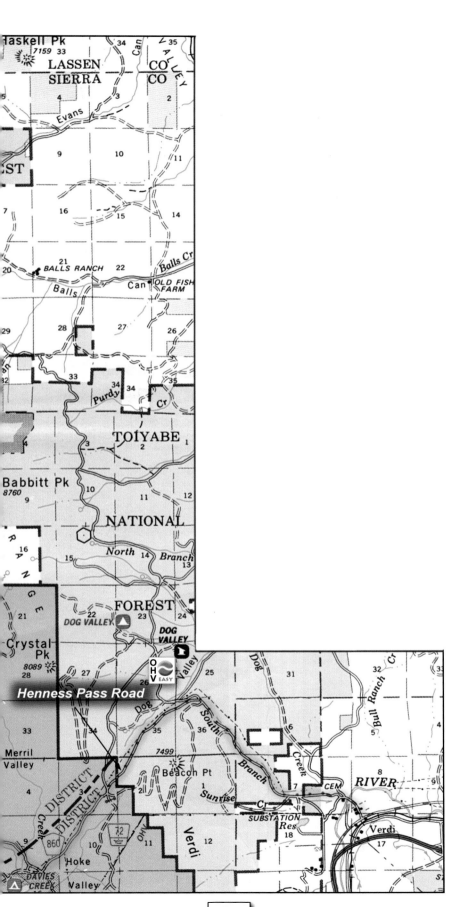

Haskell Pk
7159 33

LASSEN CO
SIERRA CO

34

35

Can VALLEY

Evans

4   3   2

9   10   11

16   15   14

7

21
BALLS RANCH   22   Balls Cr

20   Can OLD FISH
    Balls   FARM

29   28   27   26

33   34
    Purdy   34   Cr
            35

TOIYABE   1
    3   2

Babbitt Pk
8760   10   11   12
    9

NATIONAL

R
A
N
G
E

16   15   North 14 Branch
                13

FOREST

21   22   23   24
    DOG VALLEY

Crystal
Pk
8089   27   26   OHV   Valley   25   Dog   31   32   Bull Ranch Cr   33
28   EASY

Henness Pass Road

33   34   35   36   South   6   4
                Branch   5

Merril
Valley   7499   Creek   7   CEM   RIVER   8
    Beacon Pt   9

4   DISTRICT   2   1   Sunrise   7
        DISTRICT   Cr   SUBSTATION   Verdi
                            Res   18   17
Creek   72   Dog OHV
    860   10   11   Verdi 12
Hoke
DAVIES
CREEK Valley

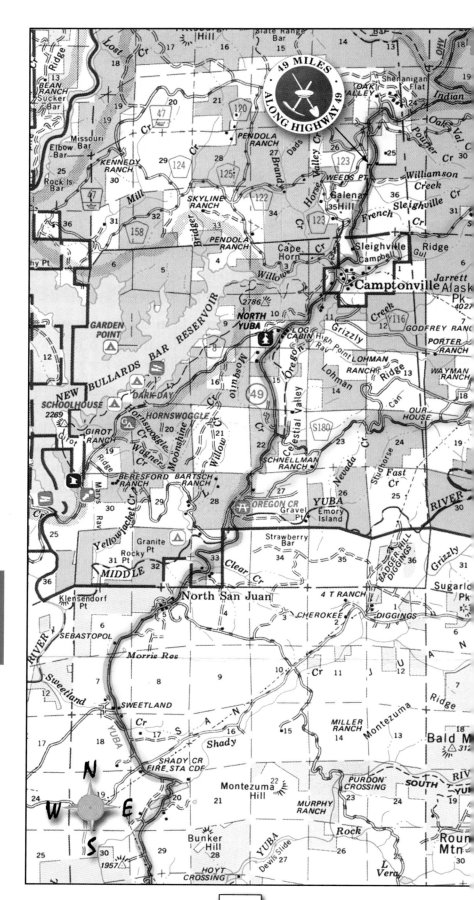

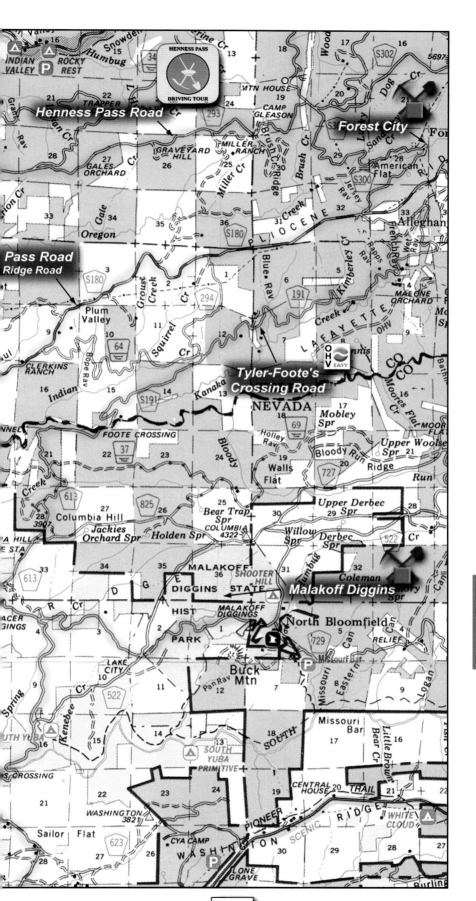

HENNESS PASS DRIVING TOUR

Henness Pass Road

Forest City

Pass Road
Ridge Road

Tyler-Foote's
Crossing Road

Malakoff Diggins

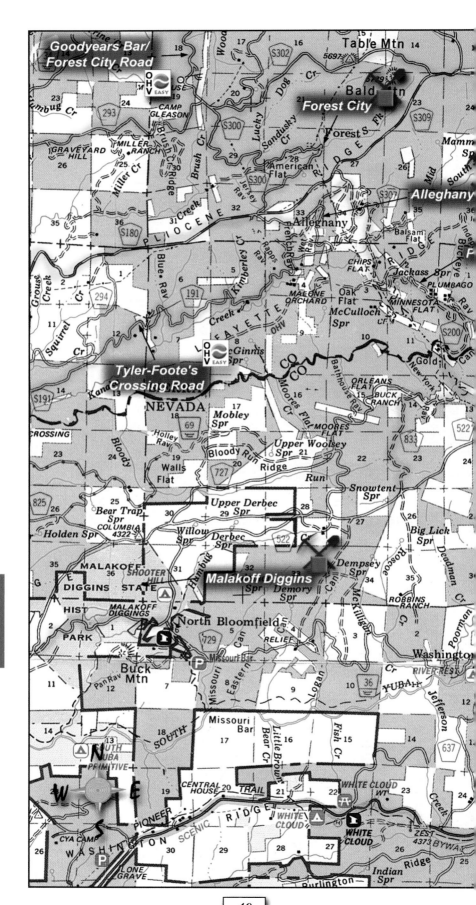

Goodyears Bar/
Forest City Road

Tyler-Foote's
Crossing Road

Malakoff Diggins

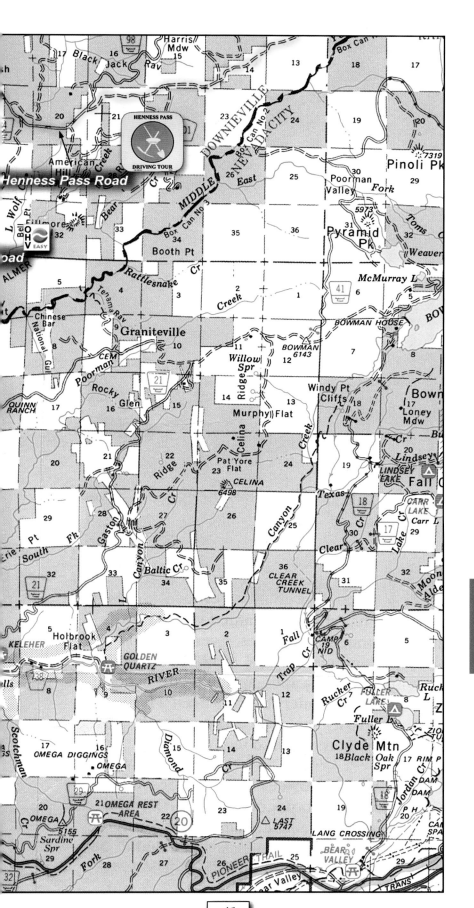

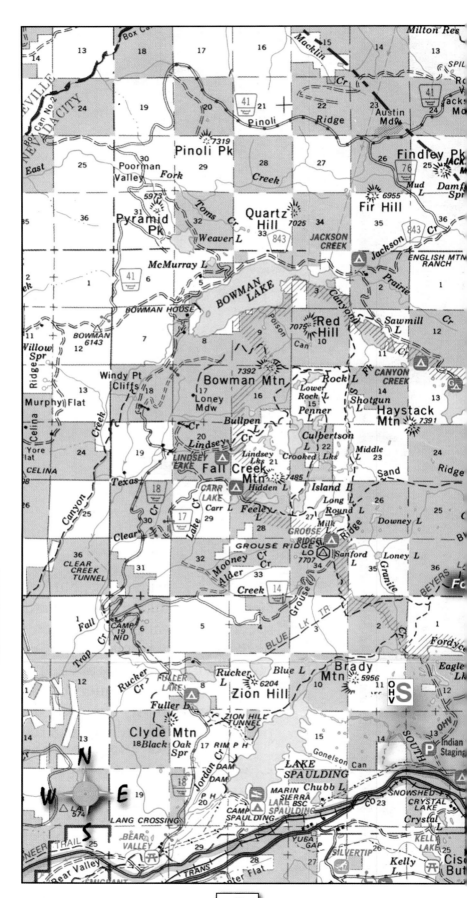

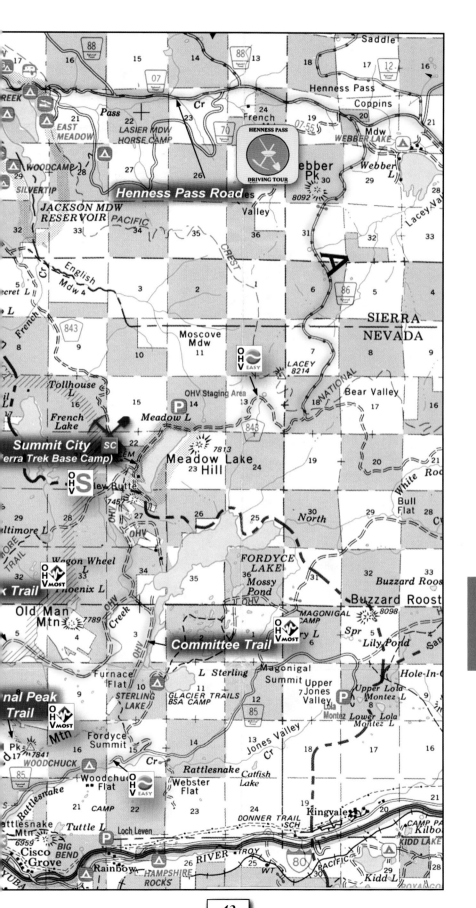

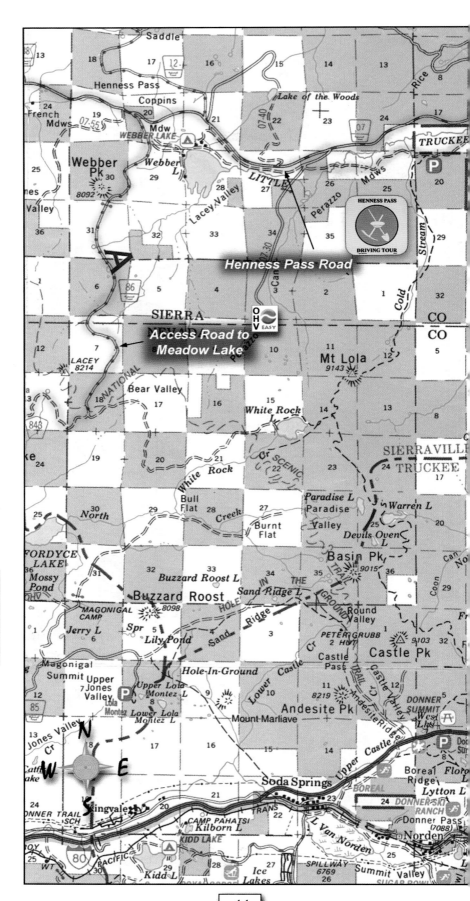

Henness Pass Road

Access Road to
Meadow Lake

HENNESS PASS
DRIVING TOUR

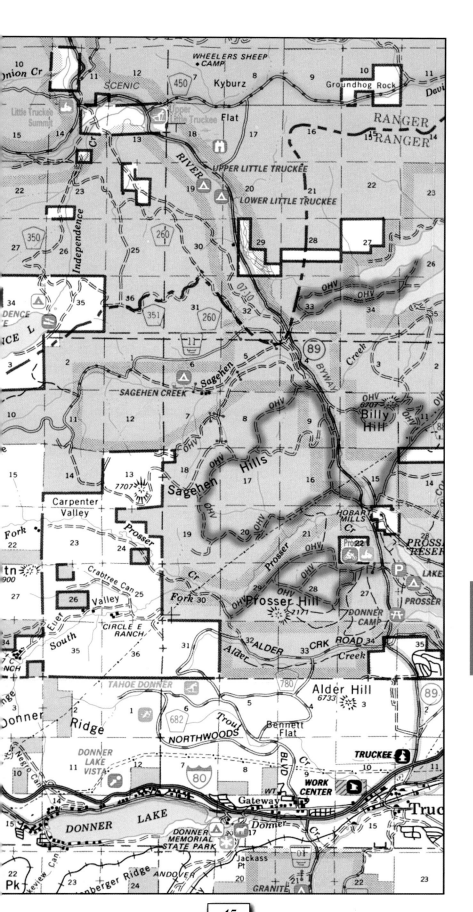

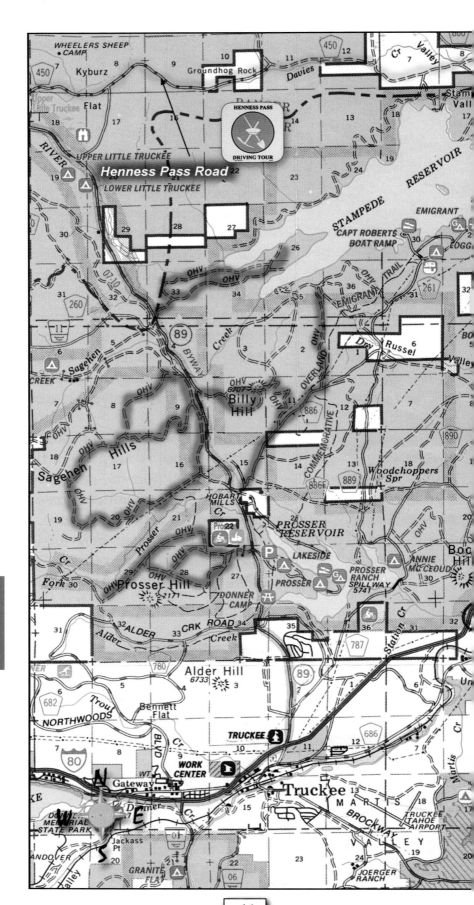

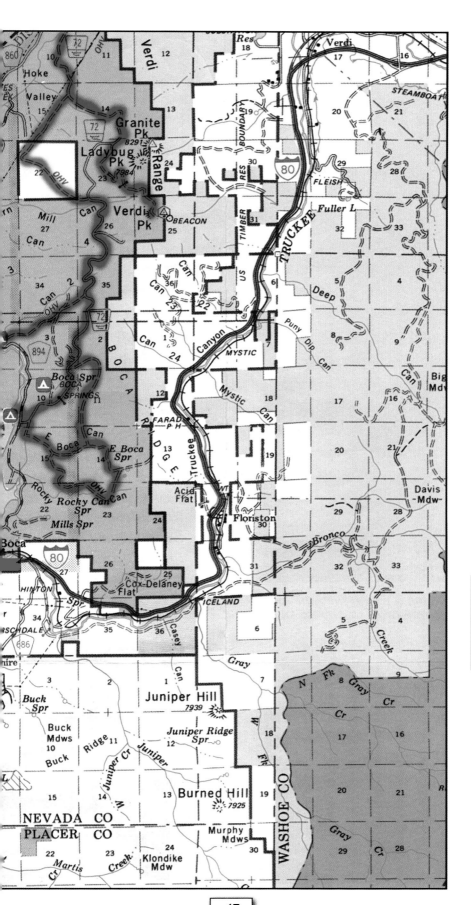

Trail Notes and *Topographic Maps*

The Tahoe National Forest straddles the Sierra Nevada between two large metropolitan areas, and encompasses one of the largest concentrations of "history" in California.

There are trails for every level of experience. There are trails for those that just want to try out their new SUV and those that want to work their rigs to the "max." Several of the trails do not need four-wheel drive at all, just a map and a willingness to explore. The key is that you enjoy the wonders, beauty, and history of one of your National Forests. These are some of the best trails in the Tahoe National Forest:

> *Bear Valley Trail*
> *Butcher Creek Trail*
> *Chimney Rock Trail*
> *Craycroft Ridge Trail*
> *Deer Lake Trail*
> *Downie River Trail*
> *Fir Cap Trail*
> *Fordyce Creek Trail*
> *Goodyears Bar/Forest City Road*
> *Gold Lake Trail*
> *Gold Valley Trail*
> *Henness Pass Road*
> *Highway 49*
> *Plumbago Road*
> *Poker Flat Trail*
> *Red Oak Canyon Trail*
> *Sierra Buttes Trail*
> *Signal Peak Trail*
> *Snake Lake and Little Deer Lake*
> *Trails*
> *Tyler-Foote's Crossing Road*

These trails are scattered all over the northern half of the Forest. Some take all day, others just a couple of hours. The key to a successful trip is that you do it safely and without damage to you, your vehicle, historical sites and the environment. Most SUV's or four-wheeled vehicles can handle the "more difficult" trials, but when you get to the "most difficult" trails, be very careful, you and your vehicle will be tested!

Bear Valley OHV Loop Trail

The Bear Valley OHV Loop Trail is located eight miles southeast of Sierraville (or 18 miles north of Truckee) with easy access from State Highway 89. Take Cottonwood Road northeast at Little Truckee Summit toward the Bear Valley Campground. There is a large staging area where you can meet and check your rig for the trek (Figure 7).

Figure 7. The Bear Valley OHV Loop Trail is a great trail for those that want to see what their rig can do. It can be a challenge, or it can be relatively easy.

Bear Valley Campground – has ten campsites large enough for motorhomes. There are toilet facilities and drinking water.

The Bear Valley Trail, generally rated as "easy," can be a nice test of your new SUV. There are a couple of tough challenges on this 20 plus-mile trail; one of the best is named "Ball Peen" a relatively new hill that will really test you and your rig. The Cottonwood Fire ravaged most of the northern half of the trail in August 1994. This fire burned over 45,000 acres. For years, users of the trail will have to contend with clearing "dead-and-down" snags (Figure 8).

The trail is usually taken clockwise, starting at the

Figure 8. The snags will be a problem for years.

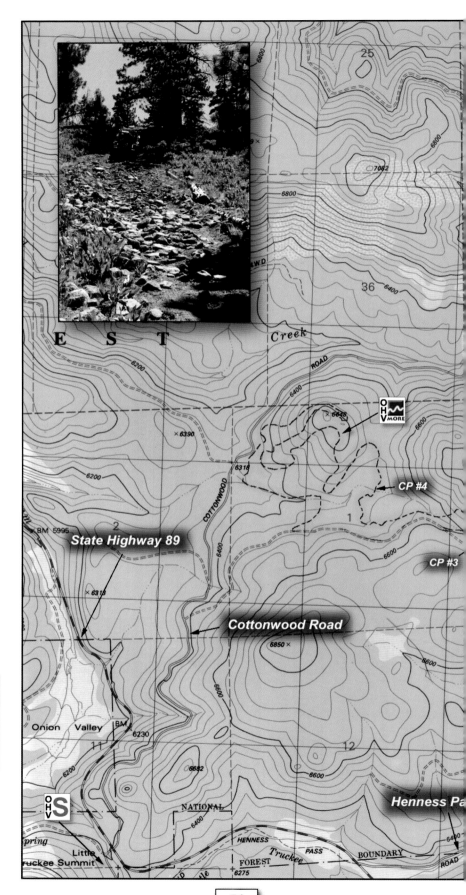

E S T   Creek

25

7082

6800

36

6390

6318

6200

BM 5995

State Highway 89

6315

Cottonwood Road

6850

6682

Onion Valley   BM 6230

11

12

pring

Little

ruckee Summit

NATIONAL

HENNESS   Truckee   PASS   BOUNDARY

FOREST   6275

OHV MORE

CP #4

CP #3

6600

8600

Henness Pa

OHV S

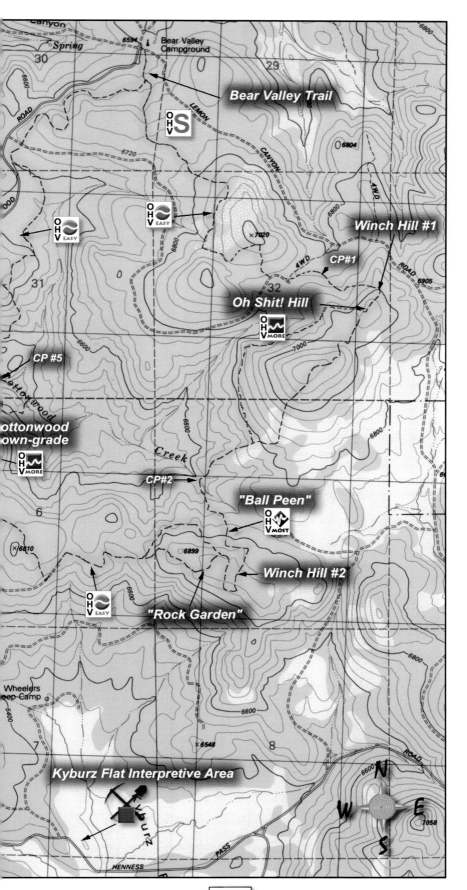

Bear Valley Campground

Bear Valley Trail

Winch Hill #1

Oh Shit! Hill

CP #5

Cottonwood down-grade

CP #2

"Ball Peen"

Winch Hill #2

"Rock Garden"

Wheelers Jeep Camp

Kyburz Flat Interpretive Area

Bear Valley Campground. Most of the first several miles will be in the old burn. Just before "CP1" you will come up on Winch Hill #1. The next obstacle is "Oh Shit! Hill," named for its ease in getting you in trouble. A little further down the trail, it splits. The trail to the left is the tougher one; the one to the right is an easy bypass. If you stay to the left, you move up the ridge where you will find some very nice views. The trails join on what was once the railroad grade used to move timber south toward Truckee.

"Ball Peen" is the next challenge (Figure 9). It is tough enough for some SUVers to be cautious and take the bypass to the left. During "Run-a-Muck" (See page 53 for more information) a fee is charged for those that want to attempt the hill; prizes are given.

Next comes Winch Hill #2 and the "Rock Garden." There is a bypass for the faint at heart. The trail now heads west, back toward Cottonwood Road. If you want to skip the last half of the trial, you can stay on the logging road near "CP3" and be on the main road in less than a mile. If you are going to complete the loop, the next several miles will be on "peak 6648." Some of the area you will travel was logged in the late 90's.

Figure 9. The "Ball Peen" can be a real challenge for you and your rig.

When you pass "CP4" and start dropping down the slope toward Cottonwood Creek, the trails drops fast. The area near the creek is "sensitive" so be sure to stay on the marked trail. The last section of the trail, from "CP5" to camp, wanders around a little, and if you don't keep a sharp eye for the trail markers, you may lose your way.

Sardine Peak Lookout – This now closed Forest Service Lookout is located several miles east of the Bear Valley Trail. The road is easy and the view is great. You can get a general feel for the topography on the Bear Valley Trail. You can also look south and view into the Kyburz area and the Henness Pass Road. Since the lookout is closed, the road is gated a short distance from the tower.

Run-a-Muck Event – This annual event, hosted by the Diablo 4 Wheeler's, is run in the middle of July. This family oriented event not only offers various four-wheel challenges, but trail games and other events. This may be a good trail and event to introduce your family to four-wheeling.

Butcher Creek Trail

The Butcher Creek Trail is one of the shortest, easiest trails in the Tahoe National Forest. This trail is rated "easy." The trail can be reached by traveling west of Packer Saddle on Forest Roads 93 and 93-3. As the road turns to the right, the trail drops off to the left toward Robinson Cow Camp. As you start down the trail, there is an outstanding cold-water spring just off the trail…stop and fill your canteens.

The trail will wind down the slope through the timber. You will approach Butcher Ranch Meadow on its southern edge. As you move around the meadow, you will cross Butcher Ranch Creek (Figure 10). Look downstream and to the left. You will see the remains of an old stamp mill. A note of caution…there are several tunnels and shafts in the area. Be careful not to stumble into one.

Figure 10. As you cross Butcher Ranch Creek, look downstream on the left and you will see an old stamp mill that was used to crush ore.

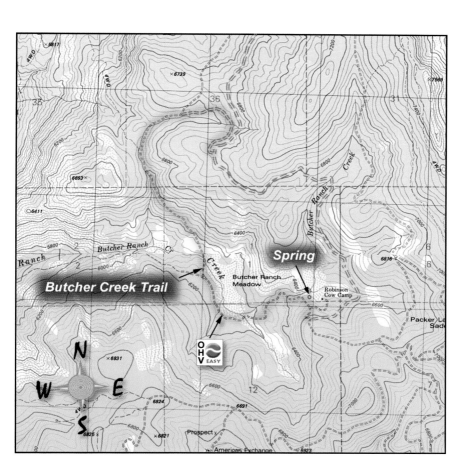

Chimney Rock Trail

The Chimney Rock Trail is located north of Downieville by about ten miles. It is a short trail, taking off to the east from the Fir Cap/Poker Flat Trail. It is short, but it is rated "more difficult" as you get closer to Chimney Rock.

To get to the Chimney Rock Trail, go north from Downieville toward Saddleback Mountain. As you climb toward the top of the ridge, you will pass such sites as Red Ant, Oak Ranch, and Saddleback Mountain and Lookout. This is one of the few remaining lookouts in the area that is staffed during the fire season; stop by and say hello.

About two miles north of the lookout, the Chimney Rock Trail branches to the right. It is a relatively short trail, that will end just west of Chimney Rock (Figure 11). From the "main road" head northeast; the trail is easy until you reach Democrat Peak, just off the trail to the north. From here the trail narrows and gets more difficult. You cannot actually drive to Chimney Rock. To see it you will have to take a short hike.

While you are in the area, take the time to visit Devil's Post Pile. It is just a short drive and hike to view this most interesting geological feature (picture inset in map to the left).

Rick Morrison

Figure 11. Chimney Rock is a basalt formation, created "many" years ago. Take the time to walk out along the ridge to view this unique geological formation.

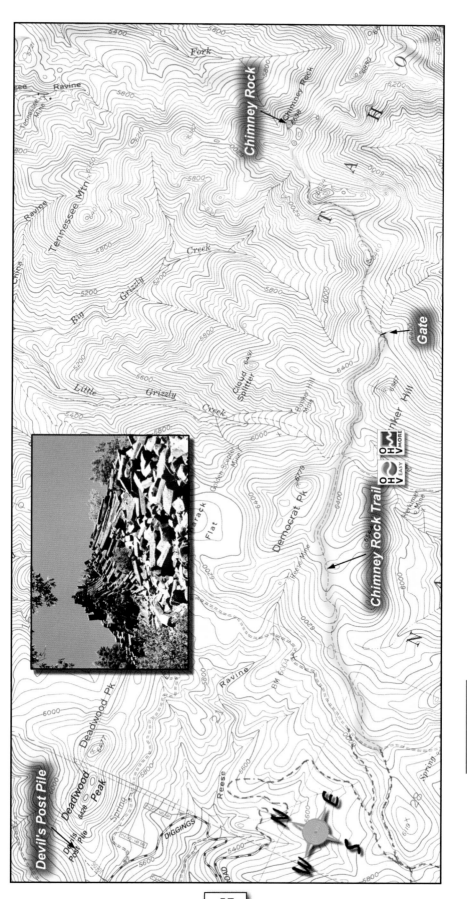

Chimney Rock

Fork

Tennessee Mtn

Ravine

Tennessee Mine

Ravine

China

Big

Grizzly

Creek

Little

Grizzly

Creek

Cloud Splitter

Bunker Hill Mine

Bunker Hill

Gate

Golden Sceptre Mine

Track

Flat

Democrat Pk
6779

Reese Mine

Experimental Mine

Chimney Rock Trail

Ravine

BM 6004

Deadwood Pk

Spring

Deadwood Peak
6697

Devil's Post Pile

Devil's Post Pile

DIGGINGS

Reese

Spring

ROAD

BM
6197

28

Craycroft Ridge Trail

The Craycroft Ridge Trail will not challenge your skills as a four-wheeler, but it will take you into some very interesting country and provide you with some spectacular views. The trail is rated "easy."

The Craycroft Ridge Trail was first used as a footpath by the 49ers to access the gold fields north of Downieville toward Poker Flat. Even today, there are active mining operations along the trail. There are caretakers that can get real "cranky" if you mess with their stuff.

You can access the trail from Downieville on County Road S514. Just after you cross the Downie River, where Pauley Creek enters the river, you will see a small sign saying "Pauley Falls." Be sure to take a minute to walk a hundred yards up the trail to view these falls.

The trail follows Pauley Creek for a some distance, and then it crosses over the ridge into Lavezzola Creek. After a mile or so, you will reach Empire Ranch and the beginning of the Craycroft Ridge Trail.

The trail moves up the west side of Empire Creek. After a little over a mile, it will switchback hard to the left. Find a wide spot and park. Walk up the creek just over a hundred yards to view one of the best virgin mixed conifer stands on the forest.

The trail will wind its way up the slope toward the ridge. You will pass though various fuel types. The trail will follow the ridge for miles, ending about a mile from Needle Point. If you take your time as you move along the trail you will see some great vistas.

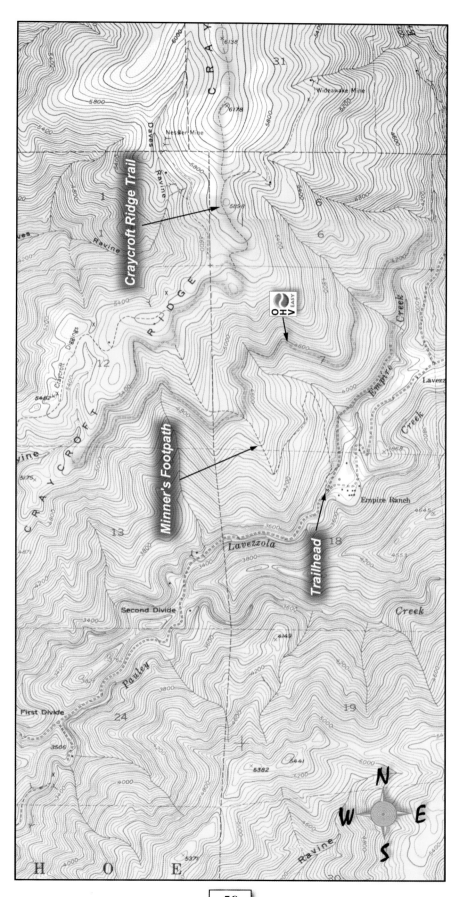

Craycroft Ridge Trail

OHV EASY

Minner's Footpath

Trailhead

Wideawake Mine

Nessler Mine

Craycroft Diggings

Empire Ranch

Lavezzola

Second Divide

Pauley

First Divide

N
W   E
S

Deer Lake Trail

Deer Lake Trail is "easy" by four-wheeler standards, but it takes you on a five-mile journey from Packer Saddle to Summit Lake. From Summit Lake you can access the Gold Lake Trail, Oakland Pond, and the Snake Lake Trail. Deer Lake Trail parallels the Pacific Crest National Scenic Trail, which is for backpackers and horses, so please stay clear of it.

As you leave Packer Saddle you move up the hill, just off the ridgeline to the left (Figure 12). You will pass through some areas that have been recently logged. There are several very nice campsites along the trail, some with great views.

Figure 12. The Deer Lake Trail is "easy" and will not be much of a challenge. As the trail moves up the ridge it parallels the Pacific Crest National Scenic Trail.

About 2½-miles from Packer Saddle, you will see Deer Lake off to the east (Figure 13). This is a beautiful lake of very clear water, fed only by the annual snowfall. There is a short trail that provides SUV access to the area just above the lakeshore. The Forest Service is very protective of

Figure 13. Deer Lake is just east of the trail. There is a trail that will take you down close to it. You will have to stop short of the lake…use the parking area.

this lake and the clarity of this "jewel" of a lake, so they will only let you get so close with your vehicle.

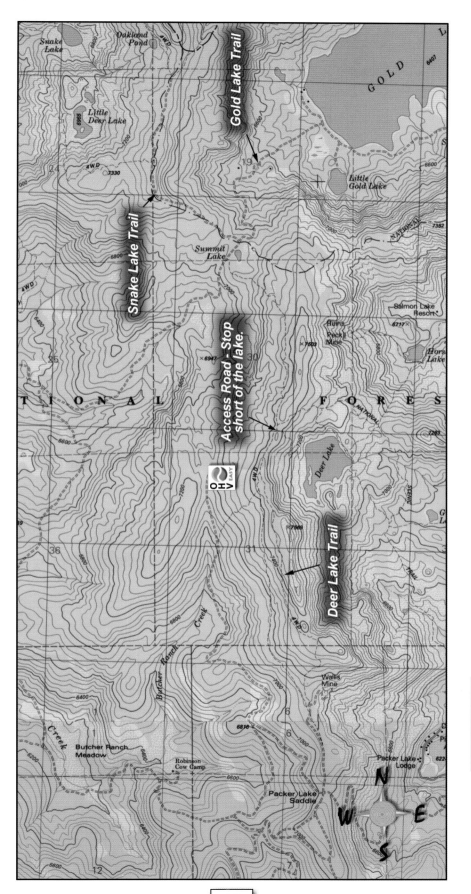

Gold Lake Trail

Snake Lake Trail

Access Road - Stop short of the lake.

Deer Lake Trail

Downie River Trail

The Downie River Trail follows the Downie River along its west bank. It is "easy" by four-wheeling standards, but one of the narrowest designated OHV trails on the forest. As you leave Downieville, stay to the left (west) side of the river. This is a very narrow trail, so narrow in some spots that you may want someone to walk in front of you to check that there isn't just "air" under your downslope tires.

The turnaround at the end of the trail isn't anything to make light of either. It is just big enough to allow one or two rigs to park. If it is "full" you may have to back out...not always an easy feat.

If you find a parking spot and want to take a hike and swim, there is a very nice swimming hole about a ½-mile up stream near the old steel bridge.

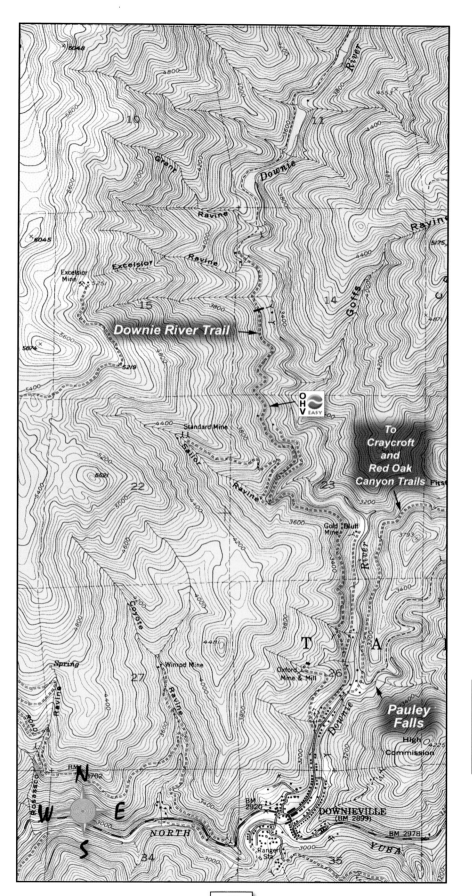

Downie River Trail

To
Craycroft
and
Red Oak
Canyon Trails

Pauley
Falls

Fir Cap Trail

The Fir Cap Trail is rated "more difficult" and is best run from the top down. The vistas are great. The Fir Cap Trail is accessed from Saddleback Road. Head west from Downieville toward Cannon Point (less than a ¼-mile), turn north on Saddleback Road. This road will take you up the ridge to Saddleback Mountain and the Poker Flat and Chimney Rock Trails.

Figure 14. Fir Cap Trail is just to the right of the bald knob. Just beyond the knob is the flat and a great vista.

As you move up Saddleback Road, you will pass through the site of Red Ant and the Monte Cristo Mine and town site. There are no buildings left, but if you look around you will find a pond, cemetery, and where the Main Street was formally located. As you reach the ridgeline, the road forks. If you continue north at the fork, you will reach Saddleback Mountain and Lookout. If you turn left, you will have the option to head toward Poker Flat, or head west back toward Highway 49 at Cal-Ida. If you turn right, you will be on the Fir Cap Trail. The trail will take you six-miles down the ridge. It will end at the road to the Excelsior Mine, just east of the Monte Cristo town site.

Figure 15. The Saddleback Mountain Lookout is a great location to view the "lay of the land."

About a mile further down the trail you will reach Fir Cap (Figure 14). This is a flat area, some 40-acres in size. The timber on this flat is classic "old growth." On the west edge of the flat, there is a great vista. Take the time to walk to the edge and take some pictures. Continue down the ridge until you reach the Excelsior Mine access road. Turn right and in less than a mile you will be back on the Saddleback Mountain Road.

Saddleback Mountain Lookout - You might want to take the time to travel about a mile north of the trailhead to visit the lookout (Figure 15) staffed by USDA Forest Service personnel during the fire season. The views are great!

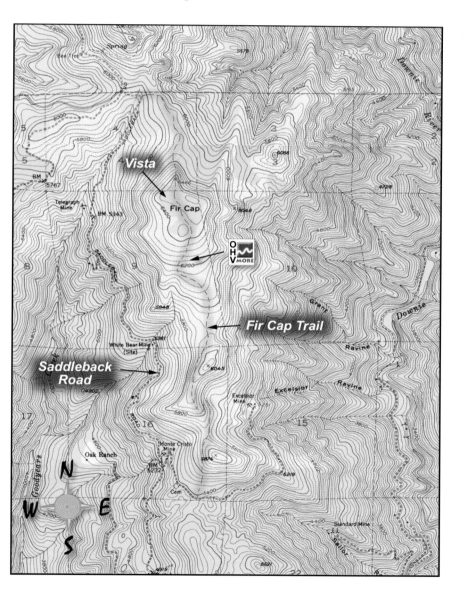

Fordyce Creek Trail

The Fordyce Creek Trail is one of the tougher four-wheel drive trails in the Sierra Nevada (Figure 16, pages 68 and 69). It seriously rivals the famous Rubicon Trail and truly meets the definition of "most difficult." Access to the southern end of the trail is from the Eagle Lakes exit off Interstate 80, just west of Cisco Grove.

(*Warning!* The Fordyce Creek Trail crosses Fordyce Creek three times. The creek is used by the Pacific Gas and Electric Company to move water from Fordyce Lake to Lake Spaulding and then to one of its hydroelectric generators. Although, the water level is reduced to safe levels for the Sierra Trek event, the streams are not safe to cross any other time of the year.)

Eagle Lakes Exit from Interstate 80 – Take the off-ramp and turn north. The paved frontage road will turn to the west. In about a half-mile you will pass the Indian Springs Campground on the left. About a 100-yards further down the road will be the access road to the Indian Springs OHV Staging area and the Signal Peak Trail.

Indian Springs Campground – The USDA Forest Service operates the Indian Springs Campground; there are 35 nice campsites with water and toilet facilities.

Indian Springs OHV Staging – This is a good spot to check your rig and lower your tire pressure before you begin your adventure. Both the Fordyce Creek Trail and the Signal Peak Trail can be accessed from here. If you are part of the Sierra Trek event, you will need to meet at their staging area about a mile further west.

Sierra Trek Staging – The Sierra Trek event uses a slightly different access route to the Fordyce Creek Trail. They cross the South Fork of the Yuba River about a mile down river from the OHV staging area. The staging area is just across the river on a parcel known as the "Patty Property," purchased with Green Sticker funds and donated to the Forest Service (Figure 17).

OHV Camping Area – Several years ago the California Association of 4Wheel Drive Clubs (CA4WDC) sponsored the development of several OHV camping sites just up the trail from the gravel bar. There are fire rings and toilet facilities.

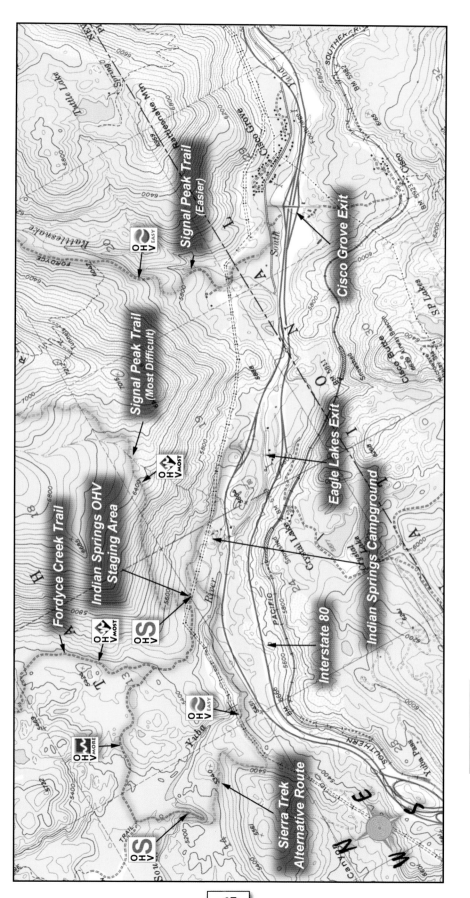

Tuttle Lake

Rattlesnake

Signal Peak Trail
(Easier)

Cisco Grove

Cisco Grove Exit

Signal Peak Trail
(Most Difficult)

Eagle Lakes Exit

Indian Springs OHV
Staging Area

Fordyce Creek Trail

Indian Springs Campground

Interstate 80

Sierra Trek
Alternative Route

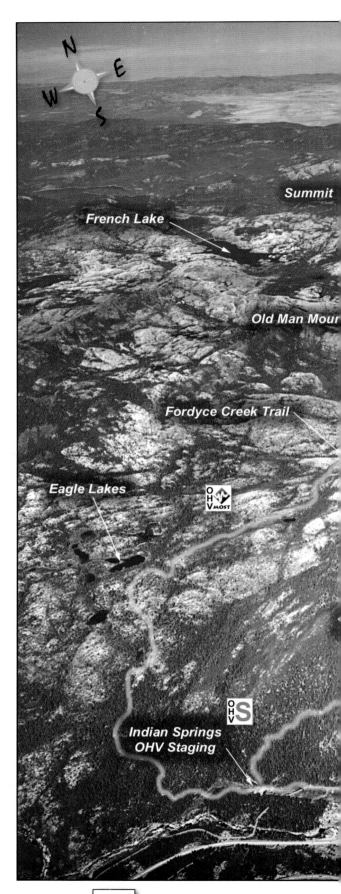

Figure 16. The Fordyce Creek Trail looking northeast from over Interstate 80. This "most difficult" trail crosses Fordyce Creek in three places, before it starts up the ridge toward Meadow Lake.

Summit

French Lake

Old Man Mour

Fordyce Creek Trail

Eagle Lakes

Indian Springs
OHV Staging

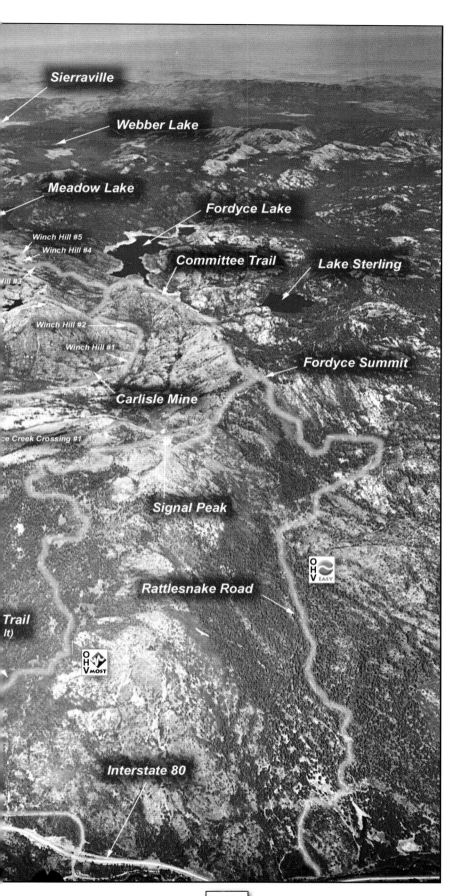

Sierraville

Webber Lake

Meadow Lake

Fordyce Lake

Winch Hill #5
Winch Hill #4

Committee Trail

Lake Sterling

ill #3

Winch Hill #2

Winch Hill #1

Fordyce Summit

Carlisle Mine

e Creek Crossing #1

Signal Peak

OHV
EASY

Rattlesnake Road

Trail
lt)

OHV
MOST

Interstate 80

Figure 17. Sierra Trek participants ready their rigs for the challenges ahead.

As you move north on the trail, the trail is fairly easy. It is narrow, rocky and moves through some nice timber. Once you join up with the trail to Eagle Lakes it gets a little rougher.

Sunrise Hill – This "more difficult" series of rock ledges is named for the fact that you are looking directly into the sun as you negotiate it in the early morning hours. You continue to move along the ridge above Fordyce Creek (Figure 18).

Figure 18. Sunrise Hill is one of the first real challenges on the trail.

As you start down toward the first creek crossing, you will weave back and forth through a series of difficult rock troughs. Just before you reach Fordyce Creek, you will have to zigzag down a steep section of the trail full of large boulders called a "sluice" (Figure 19).

Fordyce Creek Crossing #1 – As noted before, the level or flow of water in the creek is controlled by the Pacific Gas and Electric Company and subject to very quick changes in flow (Figure 20). Be very careful if you elect to cross – it may be safe now, but will it be safe in a couple of minutes? Once you cross the creek you are at its mercy, since there is no way out without crossing it again further down the trail. The trail from here to the Carlisle Mine access road is very narrow and rocky where you will find a couple of "more difficult" challenges.

Figure 19. The trail drops down toward the first crossing of Fordyce Creek.

Figure 20. This shows Fordyce Creek Crossing #1 at a "Sierra Trek Low." It normally flows several feet deeper than this.

Carlisle Mine – This mine is located to the north of the trail. It had the same fate as the other mines in the area. There was "color" in the ore, but it was hard to extract.

Winch Hill #1 – This section of the trail climbs up a seam in the rocks. It is very steep, rocky, and narrow. The real tough part is the last rock ledge at the top (Figure 21). Spectators and well wishers have a great view.

Fordyce Creek Crossing #2 – The approach to the second crossing of the creek is through an "old growth" stand of timber. Just before you reach the creek there is a significant drop (Figure 22).

Figure 21. Winch Hill #1 is a narrow chute. The last 20 feet offers two "very interesting" ledges. This Winch Hill provides one of the best spectator seats on the trail.

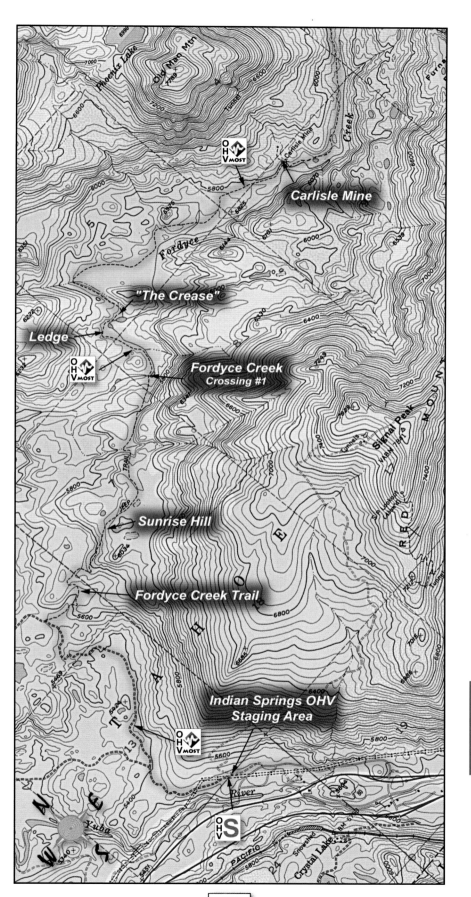

Figure 22. After the drop into the creek, you will find a large hole about halfway across the stream making for some added excitement. The water level during Sierra Trek allows for safer fording.

Winch Hill #2 – The trail moves up the hill and then hooks to the right just above a large Ponderosa Pine (Figure 23). Starting at this tree and above is where you may need some help.

Committee Trail – The Committee Trail joins the Fordyce Creek Trail just below the dam. This is where "injured rigs" are taken off the trail. Beware that crossing Fordyce Creek at this location is not as easy as it may look. You have to go up-stream a short distance

Figure 23. Winch Hill #2 provides a nice challenge. The trail moves up the hill through a boulder "sluice," hooking to the right just beyond the large Ponderosa Pine. Then it gets tough.

before you attempt to cross, or you will find out just how much water your rig can handle. Once you get up on the ridge, it is an easy run to the Cisco Grove Exit on Interstate 80. This is called the Committee Trail because it allows all of the volunteers working the event to experience the thrills of the trail, without having to run the whole route. Just past the fork in the trail, you find "The Squeeze Rock," one of the narrowest spots on the trail (Figure 24).

Figure 24. This is one of the narrowest sections on the trail. It separates the wide rigs from the narrow rigs.

Launna's Hill – As you leave the access point for the Committee Trail, you will start up the ridge. This section of the trail is steep, dusty, rocky, and "nasty," so take it easy (Figure 25).

The Grotto – This section of the trail gets its name from all the rocks and boulders. Move through it slowly as you approach Winch Hill #3.

Winch Hill #3 – As move up through this challenge, the trail will turn to the right and really narrow as you reach the top. It is said to be the "mother of all squeezes" (Figure 26).

Winch Hill #4 – This winch hill takes you through a long, uphill, twisting, boulder-filled "sluice" that will test your skill and your rig. Go slowly and easy does it!

Excelsior Mine – Just before you reach the base of Winch Hill #5, you will see several old rusty tanks. These were part of the water supply for the mine. As you pass above the most difficult part of the last challenge of the trail, you will reach a gravel road and the access to the mine (Figure 27).

Winch Hill #5 – As you pass several rusting tanks that were part of the operations at the Excelsior Mine, the trail will get steeper and take three distinct turns, all involving major challenges and delicate negotiations.

Figure 25. Launna's Hill is one of the a more difficult sections of the trail. It is loose, dusty, and rocky.

Figure 26. Winch Hill #3 is one of the better challenges on the trail. It ends with these squeeze rocks. Note the steel anchor (with the cup on it). This is used to anchor winch cables to pull vehicles over the top.

Figure 27. The trail leaves Fordyce Creek just below the dam. As you move up the ridge, there are several challenges in your future. Take it slow and easy.

Meadow Lake – Meadow Lake has a very interesting history (Figure 28). Picture thousands of people living in the meadow and a small double-decker paddleboat taking you on a Saturday night cruise around the lake. Meadow Lake is one of the best examples of "boom and bust" stories in the Sierra Nevada gold fields, but gold was not what originally brought the people to Meadow Lake. It was the need for water for the Nevada City/Grass Valley area. A dam was constructed in 1853 to raise the water level of Meadow Lake.

In the early 1860's, Henry Hartley built a cabin near Meadow Lake so he could run a trap line. In 1863, he found a red-colored outcropping in the granite about a mile

Figure 28. Meadow Lake is where Sierra Trek locates its base camp. This is a picture looking southwest from Lacey Peak.

south of the lake. He found small flakes of gold in this decomposed iron ore. In September of '63, he and two friends staked out two mining claims.

In 1865, the word got out that there was gold at Meadow Lake and the "boom" was on. Other mining operations were "panning out" so any new "find" attracted miners ready to make it rich. By spring, there were over 250 men and several women living near the lake. There were already several businesses established. By August, there were 75 homes, several stores, restaurants, boarding houses and saloons. It was estimated that 100 new people were arriving every day. The winter weather reduced the population, but by the spring of '66, there were thousands of people living in Meadow Lake, most of them fresh from the mines of Virginia City.

On March 24, 1866, the city was incorporated. By May there were 4,000 people; lots were selling, and houses and shops were being built. There were four sawmills providing lumber and the Pacific Mine said that they were averaging $53 of silver and gold to the ton. By August there were 500 buildings in town. A small double-decked steamer could be found cruising on the lake. It was reported that there were 90 saloons in town. In December, the public school opened…there were 51 students.

Assay tests for most of the claims indicated that the gold and silver was in the ore, but it proved to be very difficult to extract. Winter was early, and 3,000 people were not able to escape to warmer climates. At times the snow was 25 feet deep. Tunnels had to be built so that people could move about.

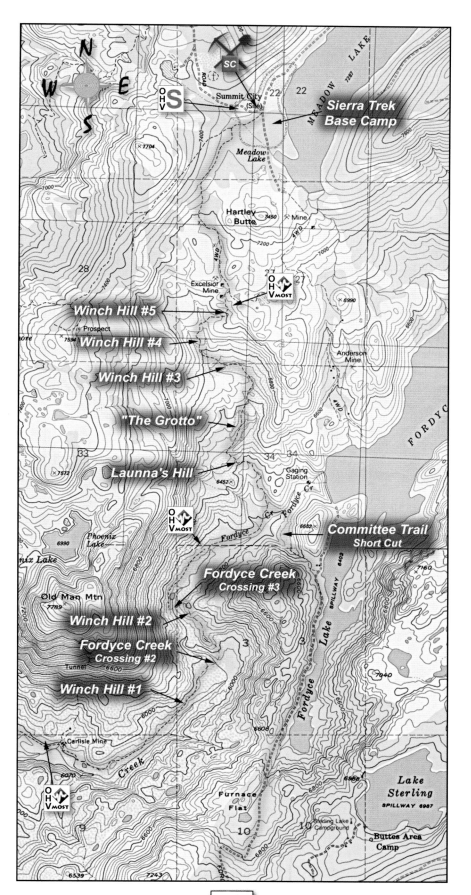

Sierra Trek
Base Camp

Meadow
Lake

Winch Hill #5

Winch Hill #4

Winch Hill #3

"The Grotto"

Launna's Hill

Committee Trail
Short Cut

Fordyce Creek
Crossing #3

Winch Hill #2

Fordyce Creek
Crossing #2

Winch Hill #1

Lake
Sterling
SPILLWAY 6987

Buttes Area
Camp

There was still hope that the mines would begin producing in the early part of 1867, but it was not to be. The ore would not yield its treasures. By September it was over, ending as quickly as it began. By June 1869, there were less than 50 people still living in the area.

Sierra Trek

The Sierra Trek event is one of the best four-wheeler's events of the summer. It is not just for those that have specially equipped four-wheel drive vehicles, but also for those that enjoy the outdoors and drive a sports utility vehicle.

The event started in the mid-1960's when members of the California Association of 4WD Clubs began hosting a family oriented four-wheel drive event in the high Sierras. What makes this event special is that it appeals to a wide range of four-wheel drive enthusiasts, not just the hard-core rock crawlers. (No one who has run the Fordyce Creek Trail will say it was a piece of cake.) It's tough, but it isn't long…it's just over ten miles, depending on who's counting and how many times they got stuck.

The event offers a beautiful camping opportunity at Meadow Lake; four-wheeling opportunities for those rigs that are under 80-inches wide. This width restriction is enforced by the committee and by several big rocks along the trail. Check with the event coordinators before registering for the event if your rig comes close to this limitation. Sierra Trek is a well-hosted family oriented event. Once you've tried it, you will very likely return.

Access to Meadow Lake from the North – The drive to Meadow Lake is a scenic trip. It will take you about an hour from Truckee, unless you are towing something big and heavy. Take State Highway 89 north from Truckee, toward Sierraville. At just over 14 miles, as you crest a ridge, you will see a sign indicating the turnoff to Independence Lake, Webber Lake, and Jackson Meadows Reservoir – turn left onto Forest Road 7. Just to your right is a Forest Service OHV staging area, with lots of parking and restroom facilities. Forest Road 7 follows the emigrant trail known as the "Henness Pass Road." It was the route used by early settlers to move into the Marysville—Yuba City area. Just past Webber Lake, the road to Meadow Lake will take off to the left.

Goodyears Bar/Forest City Road

The Goodyears Bar/Forest City Road is an "easy" route to the Henness Pass Road, Forest City, and Allegany. You can access it from Highway 49 about six miles west of Downieville. You turn north and quickly drop and cross the North Yuba River (Figure 29). As soon as you cross the river, you will begin a 2,000-foot climb to the ridgeline at Mountain House. This is where you will join with the Henness Pass Road.

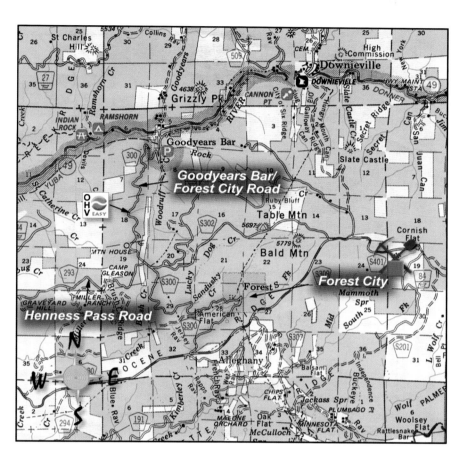

Mountain House

Mountain House, another stage stop and inn, was located at the intersection of Henness Pass Road and the road between Goodyears Bar (on Highway 49) and Forest City. The actual site of theInn is located toward the northwest on the ridge.

If you turn right you, will be on the Henness Pass Road heading toward Camptonville. If you go straight, you will be on the Henness Pass Road. In just a couple hundred yards, the road splits. The fork to the left is the historic route to what is called the "upper bifurcation." The road to the right is better and will take you to

Forest City, the southern branch of the Henness Pass Road and Alleghany.

Stage Holdup Site

It was at this site on July 1, 1887, that a bold stage holdup was attempted. A lone bandit ordered the Forest City Stage, carrying gold from the Bald Mountain Mine, to stop. But before the stage could come to a halt, the driver and "shotgun" were wounded. The

Figure 29. As you leave Highway 49, you quickly drop down to the North Yuba River. From here the road climbs 2,000 feet to its junction with the Henness Pass Road at Mountain House.

horses bolted, dragging the stage out of harms way. A posse was formed, but they were unable to apprehend the bad guy. Rumor has it that the wounds may have been caused by "friendly fire" when the fellow riding "shotgun" got a little excited with all that was going on!

Just down the road from the holdup site, you will see a trail heading off to the north. This is called the Sandusky Road. It is a short cut back to Henness Pass Road.

Forest City

Forest City was established in 1852 near a "breakout" of the "Great Blue Lead" (See page 2). The town quickly grew to 1,000 within a year (Figure 30). By then the town had seven general stores, four clothing stores, one tin shop, five hotels, two meat markets, four blacksmiths shops and five carpenter shops. Forest City is a "must" stop. The community operates a great museum in what was the dance hall—it may not be open, since volunteers staff it. (One of the locals may be able to open it for you, or if you are planning a group tour of the area, call (530) 287-3413 for assistance.)

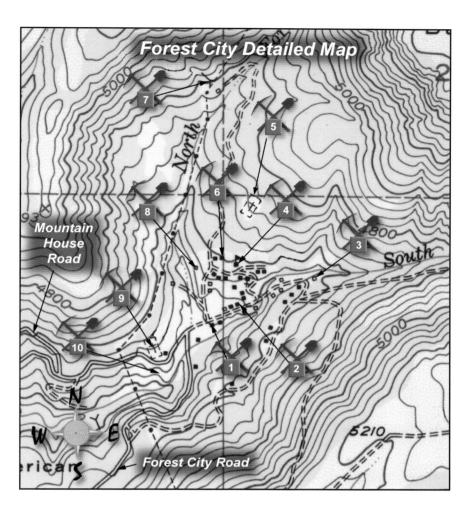

Forest City Detailed Map

Forest City is on property owned by the USDA Forest Service. It is in the National Registry of Historic Places and has special status as a historic district to protect it's cultural resources.

(1) Dance Hall (Museum) – *Built following the fire of 1883, this three-story building housed on the first floor a barbershop, saloon and billiards hall. The second floor contained a large rubber-cushioned dance floor. The third floor housed the offices of the Knights of Pythias' fraternal lodge. The structure now houses the Forest City Museum.*

(2) Forest City Meat Market – *Built by George Miller following the fire of 1883, this building housed the family in the back and a butcher shop in front.*

(3) Miller's Slaughter House *(site)* – *This is where the cows and pigs were brought for slaughter and preparation for sale at the meat market.*

Figure 30. The schoolhouse as it looked when Forest City was at its peak.

(4) Forest City Schoolhouse – *This building was constructed in 1874 (Figure 31) and housed up to 50 students until the mid 1930s. Behind the school you will find a stone-lined swimming pool.*

(5) Fuller House – *Built in 1864 by A. G. Fuller, a miner and water ditch owner, the house was originally a smaller cabin constructed with no framing, just two layers of crisscrossed 1 by 12-inch planking (Figure 32).*

(6) Pioneer Cemetery – *The pioneer cemetery is located on a flat on the hill above the schoolhouse.*

Figure 31. The schoolhouse as it looks today. Be sure to visit the site and locate the old stone-lined swimming pool.

(7) North Fork Mine – This was one of the earliest mines in the area. Much of the early machinery can be seen scatted around the yard. This mine is still being worked, so it is off limits to visitors.

Figure 32. The Fuller home; one of the typical homes in Forest City. It is located just to the west of the school house.

(8) Bald Mountain Mine (site) – Production started in 1872 and for 15 years it was the greatest "drift," or

Figure 33. The Bald Mountain Mine used this engine to move gravel from the mine. This picture was taken in the late 1870s.

underground gravel mine, in California. Over 250 miners were employed during it's peak years (Figure 33).

(9) Mountain House Cemetery – Established by the Odd Fellows in 1864.

(10) Chinese Cemetery – Forest City had a significant Chinese population through the 1890's. The Chinatown was located in the canyon directly below town.

Gold Lake Trail

The Gold Lake Trail is a "more difficult" trail, and is one of the bumpiest you will find. This trail is on the Plumas National Forest, but it provides an alternate route to and from some of the best trails in the Tahoe National Forest.

If you are going to use the trail to access the various trails west and south of Gold Lake, take the Gold Lake Road (County Road 620/519) north from Highway 49 at Bassetts. Turn left toward the boat-launching ramp.

Gold Lake has an interesting history. Thomas Stoddard, a Scottsman who served as a sailor on the HMS Asia, and later as schoolmaster and editor of a paper in Pennsylvania, showed up in Marysville and Nevada City with some gold and a story of a lake full of it for the taking. Word of his find spread like wildfire. In May 1850 he told everyone he was going back to the lake. By the time he reached North Yuba River, the "expedition" had reach a thousand prospectors. From a ridge overlooking a large lake (the date was June 14, 1850), he said that it "looked like the one." That was enough! In the end, however, this no-name lake that didn't have any gold.

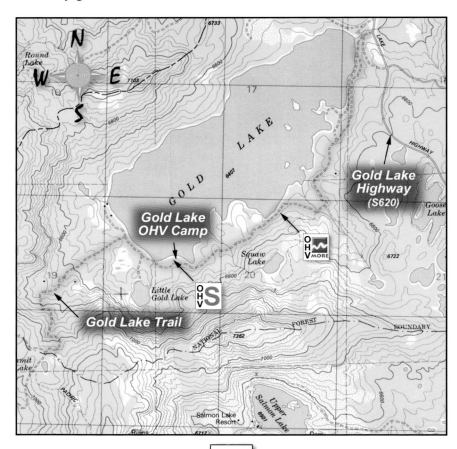

The whole story was fabricated by Stoddard and reinforced by newspaper reporters citing assay reports of great wealth, but there was no gold. In honor of this event, those that got sucked in on the fraud, named Stoddard's lake, Gold Lake.

The Gold Lake Trail will take you along the south shore of the lake (Figure 34). There is an OHV campground about three miles in. It is a nice spot, but the wind really "hums" from the north every afternoon, so plan all of your lakeside activities for the mornings. There is a short spur trail that takes you up to Little Gold Lake.

On the south end of the lake, the trail takes a turn to the left. It wanders up the slope toward Summit Lake and access to the Snake Lake Trail, Deer Lake Trail, and Gold Valley.

Figure 34. Gold Lake as seen from the ridge near Summit Lake.

Graeagle

Snake Lake Trail

Snake Lake

Gold Valley Trail

Gold Valley

Deer Lak

Smith Lake Trail

Butcher Creek Trail

Butcher Ranch
Meadow

Clio

Gold Lake

Gold Lake Trail

Deer Lake

Packer Lake

Sierra Buttes Trail

Gold Valley Trail

The Gold Valley Trail is rated as "more difficult," not so much for the trail itself, but the access to it will present some challenges.

Gold Valley is one of those places that if you've been there you want to keep it a secret. If you did not know it was there, you would miss it. There are three ways to access it. The most challenging is via the Snake Lake Trail. This trail is noted "most difficult," so be prepared for challenges.

The easiest access is from Packer Saddle. Take the road west from Packer Saddle past the south access point for the Butcher Creek Trail. You will eventually come to a wide-open spot where the road forks. If you stay to the right, you will eventually wind up at Summit Lake above Gold Lake. If you turn left and start down the hill, you will be on the access road to Gold Valley.

As you proceed down the slope you will pass the access road to the Empire Mine. This is private ground and well patrolled. The road is a little rough, but nothing you cannot handle if you go slowly.

Once you reach the valley floor, the road splits. If you go left (down stream) you will be able to follow the creek for a mile or so. You can also access the Smith Lake Trail (Figure 35) which is a trail worth taking the time to explore. While you are in the area, take

Figure 35. The trail to Smith Lake is a little rough, especially on the short pitch to the lake itself.

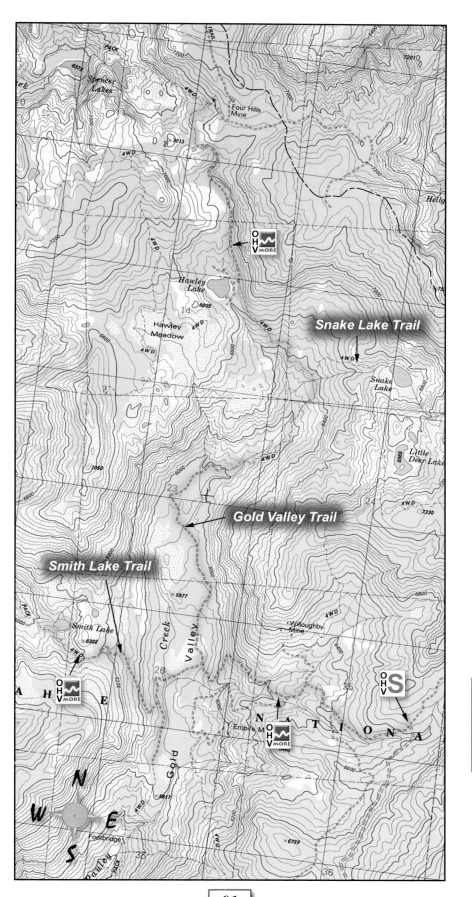

time to explore the trail to the Big Boulder Mine.

If you turn north when you first reach the valley, the trail will take you up along Pauley Creek toward Hawley Lake (Figure 36). Pauley Creek is the same one that flows into the Downie River at Downieville. Less than a ¼-mile up the trail, where it turns sharply right, you will see a trail to the left. This is the access to a nice campsite. It is large enough for several tents and is right alongside the creek. There is plenty of evidence that this was a favorite summer camping site for the Maidu. There are more nice campsites further up the trail.

Figure 36. The Gold Valley Trail takes you through some very nice old-growth timber. Take your time to really "visit" this great place.

Once back on the trail, you will cross the creek twice before you start up the slope. Just as you leave the valley, there is a short steep pitch that takes you over the roots of a large Douglas fir. This is known as "Glenn's Bench." Just past this point you will see the access to the Snake Lake Trail.

About a mile up the trail from the Snake Lake Trail, you will approach Hawley Lake. The lake and meadow are privately owned by the Boy Scouts of America. The trail eventually reaches the ridgeline and the northern boundary of the Tahoe National Forest. You can continue on to the north on roads that will eventually take you to Highway 89 and Graeagle.

Henness Pass Road

Henness Pass Road is not going to challenge your four-wheel drive skills since it is a well-traveled county-maintained road.

In 1849, Joseph Zumwalt originally pioneered the Henness Pass route, as he traveled east from his mining claim on the Downie River, in an attempt to "salvage" items left behind by the emigrants. The route was then designed and constructed by Patrick Henness in the early 1850's. By 1852, the road was in heavy use.

The Henness Pass Road really came into favor when silver was discovered in Nevada. Supplies were moved up the Sacramento River to Marysville and then hauled overland to the Comstock mines near Virginia City. The traffic was so heavy at times, it was suggested that freight wagons travel by day and passenger stagecoaches by night. Freight traffic practically stopped overnight when the railroad link was completed in 1868.

Oregon Creek Covered Bridge

This site is where Oregon Creek meets the Middle Yuba River (Map Reference #1). The Maidu used this area as a seasonal campsite for hundreds of years. In 1871 the covered bridge was constructed. In 1883, a dam located upstream on the Middle Yuba River ruptured moving debris down stream. This debris formed a new dam and lake just downstream of the bridge. The floodwater lifted the bridge, causing it to float downstream about 150 feet. It was subsequently repositioned, but reversed from its original alignment (Figure 37).

Camptonville

Gold was first discovered in the Camptonville area in 1852 (Map Reference #2). By 1857 hydraulic-mining operations were in full swing. Water was moved into the area from Webber Lake via the 67-mile Truckee Ditch. The ditch terminated at Sleighville House, the next stop on the Henness Pass Road.

As you enter Camptonville, on the left you will notice a monument to Lester Pelton (Figure 38). Pelton was a carpenter that lived in Camptonville. In 1879 he designed a new split-bucked waterwheel that proved to be twice as efficient as existing waterwheels in its ability to harness the power of moving water. Pelton's wheels were used to power stamp mills, flourmills and later, electrical generators. The Pelton Wheel design is still used to this day. Just behind the Pelton Wheel, you can see the old Camptonville jail. Its last "resident" was Ralph Rogers. Mr. Rogers was noted for his ability to make noise.

Figure 37. The Oregon Creek Covered Bridge provides access to the southern route of the Henness Pass Road. It was repositioned after being washed off its foundation.

During his last stay in jail, he made so much noise that the jailer simply let him go, rather than have him disrupt the community any longer.

Camptonville started as a gold-mining community, but ended up as a freight staging area, complete with warehouses to store goods during the winter months. The Henness Pass Road was usually open from March to November.

Figure 38. A monument to Lester Pelton, whose waterwheel design is used today. Just behind the wheel is the Camptonville Jail.

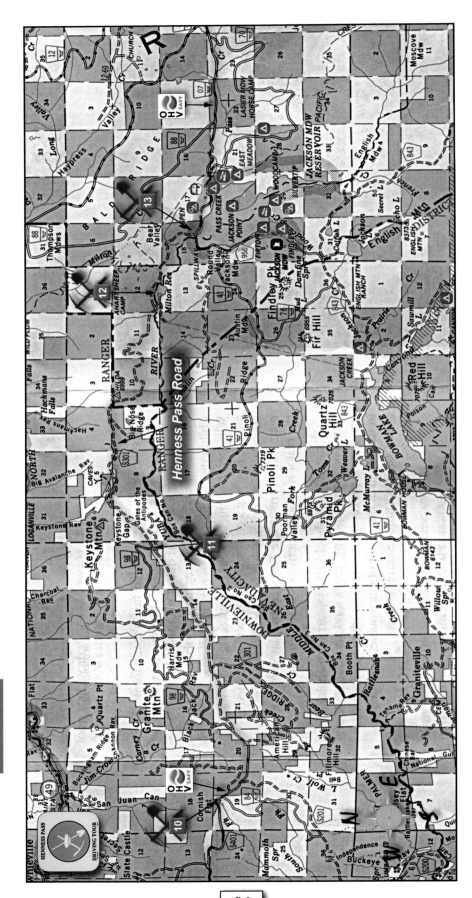

Sleighville House

Sleighville House (Map Reference #3), a stage stop and inn, was built in 1849. It is located at the 4,000-foot level. During the winter, wagons were exchanged for sleighs to travel over the snow. This was also where the tolls were collected for the stretch of road east to Mountain House. The reservoir that stored water from Webber Lake is off to the right. From here, starting in about 1852, the Sierra Nevada Lake and Water and Mining Company, moved water via ditch and flume to the hydraulic mining operations down slope in Camptonville. As you move up the ridge, there are several spots where you can view sections of the old Truckee Ditch below the road. However, the system of ditches and flumes lost so much water, it never proved profitable, and the company was in business for less than five years.

Negro Tent

Negro Tent (Map Reference #4) opened for business in 1850. It was another stage stop and inn that "serviced" the many travelers through the area. It is said that this was a gathering place for "bad men and bad women." This site went by several names, Hollow Log and Sierra-Nevada House. It remained open until 1888, when it burned to the ground. Some of the old wagon road is visible just east of here (Figure 39).

Graveyard Hill

As you move up the ridge you see a cross just above the road, but this marker is a hoax (Map Reference #4a). No one in his or her right mind would attempt to bury someone in that "volcanic cement." The actual graveyard site is out-of-site, just up the road.

Miller Ranch

The Miller Ranch (Map Reference #4b), just off the road to the south, was used to grow produce for the many travelers and their livestock.

Gleason Spring

This was a favorite spot for people and animals to "water" and rest (Figure 40). It was named for a telephone line repairman who died near here (Map Reference #4c).

Mountain House

Mountain House, another stage stop and inn, was located at the intersection of Henness Pass Road and the road between Goodyears Bar (on Highway 49) and Forest City. The site of the inn is located toward the northwest on the ridge (Map Reference #5).

If you turn left, you will drop down toward the North Yuba River and Highway 49. If you turn right, you will be continuing on the Henness Pass Road. In just a couple hundred yards, the road splits. The fork to the left is the historic route to what is called the "upper bifurcation." The better road is to the right, it will take you to Forest City, the southern branch of the Henness Pass Road and Alleghany.

Stage Holdup Site

It was at this site on July 1, 1887, that a bold stage holdup was attempted (Map Reference #5a). See page 79 for the details of the event.

Figure 39. A section of the old road near Negro Tent.

Forest City

Forest City was established in 1952 near a "breakout" of the "Great Blue Lead" (Map Reference #6). See pages 79 through 82 for more information on Forest City.

Lower Bifurcation

This is where the roads to Forest City and Alleghany cross the Pliocene Ridge Road, once known as the southern branch of the Henness Pass Road (Map Reference #7).

Figure 40. This historic spring and water trough was used to water the thousands of travelers that passed along the Henness Pass Road.

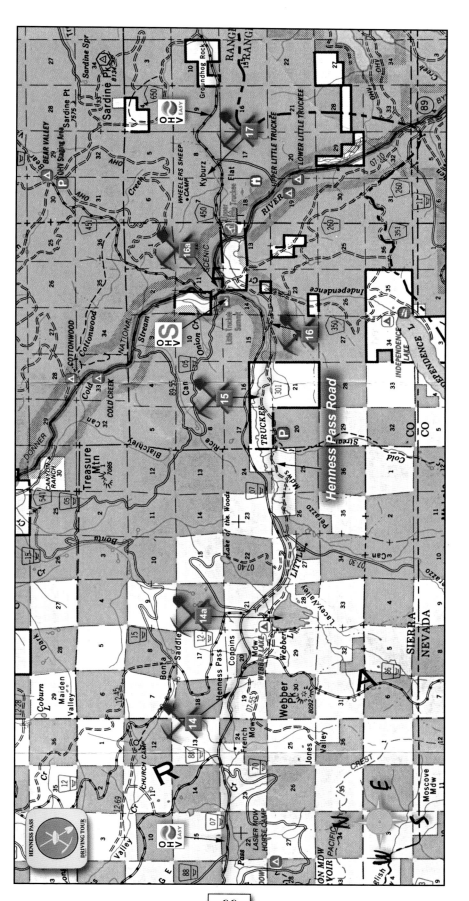

Fred's Ranch

This is the site of a stage stop and ranch and the intersection of an old road connecting Forest City and Alleghany. In those days you could see both mining communities from the ridge (Map Reference #8).

Upper Bifurcation

This is where the northern and southern branches of the Henness Pass Road meet (Map Reference #9).

Cornish House

In 1861, a stage stop and inn were constructed. There was a gold mine about a mile northeast of the site. This site was also known as Nebraska Flat, Nebraska City, and Nebraska Diggings (Map Reference #10). About a mile east of Cornish House, the pavement ends and the road splits. If you stay to the right, you will be on the Henness Pass Road. Both roads will take you to Middlewaters.

Middlewaters

The stage stop and inn was open for business in the early 1860's (Map Reference #11).

Milton Reservoir

This is the site of the community of Milton. Water from the lake was moved via a ditch to Nevada City (Map Reference #12). In the 1920's, a tunnel was constructed to carry the water through the mountain to Bowman Lake.

Jackson Meadows

In the early 1850's, Henness was part owner of a ranch that harvested hay from the meadow (Map Reference #13). What was once referred to as "the finest three-storied building that you can find outside of town" is now under water in Jackson Meadows Reservoir.

Henness Pass

At 6,920 feet, this is one of the lowest passes through the Sierra (Map Reference #14). It was named for Patrick Henness. Just east of the pass you will see Forest Road 86 on the right. This is the access to Meadow Lake and the north end of the Fordyce Creek Trail.

Webber Lake

Originally named Truckee Lake, this natural lake supplied water to hydraulic mining operations in Camptonville (Map Reference #14a). In 1860, Dr. David Webber, moved from Downieville and built a small hotel near the lake. He turned this hotel and lake into what may have been the first "resort" in the northern Sierra. People from the Sacramento Valley and Virginia City traveled to the Webber Lake to relax and enjoy natural vistas of the northern Sierra.

Davis Station

Not much is left of this once stage stop and inn (Map Reference #15). If you look closely, you will be able to see the foundation of the main house and corral, and some signs of an old foundation where the barn stood.

Independence Intersection

This is an interesting site where you can get a real feel for what the Henness Pass Wagon Road really looked like (Map Reference #16). About $1/_{10}$ of a mile south of the present day Henness Pass Road, on the road to Independence Lake, you will be able to view some of the historic road. Be sure to stop and view this site.

Little Truckee Summit

This summit is one foot less than 6,400 feet above sea level (Map Reference #16a). Just to the left of the intersection of Forest Road 07 and/or the modern day Henness Pass Road and State Highway 89, is a major OHV staging area. It is most heavily used during the winter.

Kyburz

Humans have used this site for over 2,000 years (Map Reference #17). The Washoe Indians used the meadow as a summer encampment while they were hunting, fishing, and gathering berries and other foodstuffs. The emigrants of the 1850's used it as a stage stop and inn and Basque sheepherders used the area in the early 1900's. The Forest Service has established the Kyburz Flat Interpretive Area as an aid in educating the public on the historic significance of the area.

Junction House

This site is at the junction of Henness Pass Road and the Sierraville Road (Map Reference #18). The ranch that was established here in the 1860's has long vanished. If you turn north on County Road 650, you will pass the access road to Sardine Lookout and the Bear Valley Trail.

Sardine House

Located in Sardine Valley, the Sardine Ranch was established here in 1865 (Figure 41). There was a barn and hotel on this site until the 1920's (Map Reference #19). County Road 860 heads to the north toward Loyalton and access to the Babbitt Peak Trail.

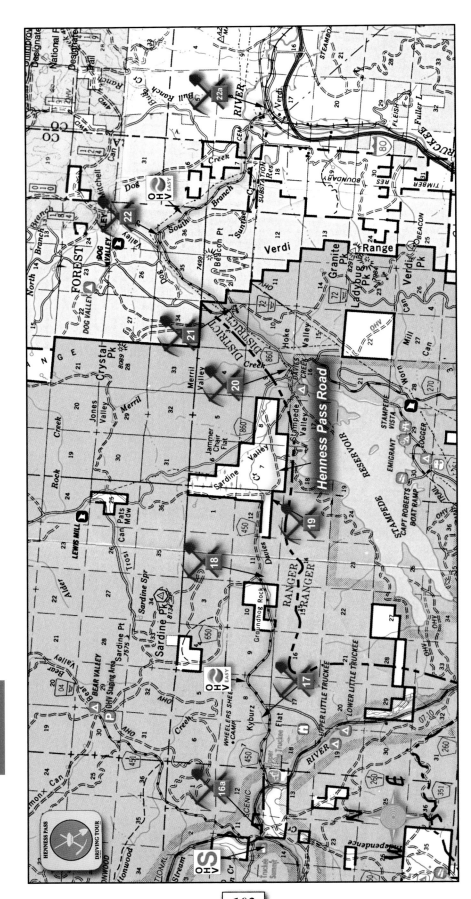

620 Stage Stop

In the 1860's this was yet another site of a hotel and stage stop (Map Reference #20). If you turn right on County Road 270 you can work your way south to the Boca Hill Trails and Interstate 80.

Second Summit

At just over 6,500 feet, this was the second summit to be climbed when traveling east to west (Map Reference #21). If you turn right you will be on the Verdi Peak Trail. It should be mentioned that this section of the Henness Pass Road was also part of the Lincoln Highway in 1915, the first east to west continental highway in the Nation. Note: This section of the Henness Pass Road was used as an alternate route for US Highway 40, when the Truckee River flooded and closed the highway.

Figure 41. This is a view of Sardine Valley from the Verdi Peak Trail. The modern day lake is Stampede Reservoir.

First Summit

This summit is 6,155 feet above sea level (Map Reference #22). The route up and over this ridge into Dog Valley was much easier than trying to navigate up the Truckee River Canyon. This route was first used in 1845. A stage stop and hotel was established here in the 1860s. You will cross into Nevada as you near Verdi.

Verdi

This is where the emigrant trail turned northwest away from the Truckee River Canyon (Map Reference #22a). Interstate 80 can be easily accessed from here.

State Highway 49

State Highway 49 extends the full-length of the historic gold country of the Sierra Nevada. It starts at Highway 41 at Oakhurst (Madera County) and extends several hundred miles to the north, ending at Highway 70 at Vinton (Plumas County). This guide covers that part of this beautiful route from State Highway 49's northern gateway, Grass Valley.

Grass Valley

Grass Valley is one of the most well preserved historic downtowns in the gold country. The town was known as the "Boomtown that never died," due to the fact that most of the gold taken from the area was from hard rock mines. George Knight on Gold Hill discovered the first hardrock mine in 1850.

The first record of European visitors to the area was in 1846, when Claude Chana and his party of French emigrants passed through the area. In 1849 when a party of emigrants stopped to refresh the animals after a tough journey across the Sierra Nevada, they named the site where they rested, Grass Valley. The first to settle in the area were a group of miners from Oregon who moved north from Coloma in late 1849.

Nevada City

The "upper crust" of the area lived in Nevada City. This well-preserved town is known as "The Queen City of the Northern Mines." The first to pan for gold in the area was John Marshall, the same person that first spotted gold at Sutter's Mill. The first cabins were constructed along Gold Run, just south of Deer Creek and the present town site. Mr. Stamps, the first "alcalde", named the town Nevada. ("Alcalde" is Spanish for chief administrative and judicial officer of a town, and "Nevada" is Spanish for snowy). In 1851, when Nevada became a state, the city of Nevada raised a stink that they had the name first. It was too late to change the name of the new state, so the city changed their name to Nevada City.

As gold became hard to find in the local streams, the miners began digging up the streets of Nevada City. No laws prevented it, but one day a local merchant stopped the practice on his street with his "six gun." In this case, "local law" prevailed.

Another first for the gold country was the introduction of electric lights to the mansions along Nevada and Prospect Streets by, what was later to become, the Pacific Gas and Electric Company.

South Yuba River

About six miles north and west of Nevada City, State Highway 49 winds down and crosses the South Yuba River. This site is now a state park that has one of the longest wheelchair accessible trails in the Nation, the Independence Trail, just off the highway on the south side of the river.

North San Juan

A German miner named Christian Kientz, named the site in the early 1850's. He named the site San Juan Hill after a site in Mexico that reminded him of an area around an old Mexican prison, San Juan de Ulloa. This name lasted until 1857 when the Postal Service wanted to build a post office. They told the community that they already had a San Juan in California, in San Benito County. The community tacked on the designation of "north" making it North San Juan.

One of the claims in the area was named "Dead Man's Claim." It was named by the locals after two young miners were killed in a cave-in in January 1853. The town is also known for having one of the first "gold brick" swindles. This type of swindle occurs when a miner claims to have a huge nugget and is loaned money when in reality they have a gold plated hunk of lead.

On August 5, 1859, a flume was completed to North San Juan from the lakes around present Bowman Lake. This incredible feat marked the beginning of a decade of great prosperity for the town and its several thousand inhabitants. Since water was the vital element in hydraulic mining, the town soon became the headquarters for numerous water companies that supplied the mines, some of whose water crossed Main Street in elevated flumes.

Three major fires swept through North San Juan during its mining days, each one wiping out most of the town. The resilient townsfolk refused to give in to the fires and always rebuilt, as long as the gravels continued to pay. At one time many houses were scattered on the hill above town. But, when it was discovered they were on top rich gravels, the mining companies wasted no time in buying them up and washing them away.

Oregon Creek

A couple of miles north of North San Juan, the Oregon Ridge Road takes off to the northeast. Just after you leave State Highway 49 you will cross Oregon Creek on the now famous bridge. This route is also the beginning of the southern branch of the Henness Pass Road. See the section on the Henness Pass Road for the history of this "backwards" bridge. (See page 90 for more details.)

Camptonville

Camptonville is just a ¼-mile off the present-day highway, so be sure to stop and view the jail and monument to "the wheel." Comptonville started its existence as a stage stop on the road to Downieville. But, in 1852, gold was discovered in the area and prosperity came to town. Before long, settlements began springing up all over the area, as the yellow metal was being discovered left and right. The prospectors had located a portion of the rich Blue Lead, an ancient river channel loaded with gold. And luckily for the miners, the deposits were covered with only a shallow layer of dirt and rock, unlike some other channels which lay hundreds of feet below the surface. (See page 90 for more details.)

The wealth of new camps brought hundreds of miners into the region in 1852, one of whom was a blacksmith named Robert Campton. Due to his popularity with the miners, the camp he settled in was christened Camptonville. A post office was established here on February 18, 1854, and by the following year the population of the town and vicinity had reached some thirteen hundred people. With the introduction of hydraulic mining in the late 1850's, the town boomed. A mile-long plank road formed the town's main street, lined on both sides by more than thirty stores, several hotels, boarding houses, offices, and a plethora of saloons.

Jouberts Diggins

Jouberts Diggins is one of many hydraulic mining operations in the area. This one is unique in that after the Sawyer Decision of 1884 that stopped most of these kinds of operations, it installed debris dams and continued operation until 1941.

Convict Flat

This campground is on the site of a camp established in the early years by the California Department of Transportation. Inmates from the State's prison system were housed here while they built this section of State Highway 49 was built. Several northern California highways were constructed using inmate labor. State Highway 299, from Redding to Arcata was another one that used inmates to do the work.

Indian Rock

The Nisenan used this site as one of their summer base camps. They gathered acorns and ground them into flour. The flour was then packed into baskets for "leaching" to remove the tannic acid and then cooked using hot rocks.

Goodyears Bar

Two brothers, Miles and Andrew Goodyear, and several other miners, discovered gold on this site in the summer of 1849. They found a rich deposit and began building what was to become Goodyears Bar. Miles died in November of 1849. Andrew wrapped his brother in a buffalo robe and buried him in an old rocker on a point opposite the bar, where he remained until his brother took his bones to Benicia, his final resting place.

Miles Goodyear, a native of Connecticut had come west with a missionary party led by Dr. Marcus Whitman, who was on his way to establish a mission along the Columbia River. After a falling out with the good doctor, Miles headed off into the wilderness and eventually settled down in the Utah Territory. When the Mormons arrived a couple of years later, Miles left and joined his brother in California and began prospecting.

The miners in Goodyears Bar suffered during the winter of 1849-50 as snowfalls came earlier and were deeper. Food became scarce, as supply trains could no longer reach the town. When parties from the outlying camps came in with the hopes of purchasing supplies, they found what little there was to buy (e.g., food, tools, or blankets) sold for the same price, $4 a pound. Many left for lower ground to wait out the winter.

The area grew so fast between the years of 1850 and 1852 that the claims staked along the Yuba River, Woodruff and Rock Creeks formed an unbroken chain, which rivaled Downieville in importance. Goodyears Bar had all the trappings of civilization; express office, saloons, stores, hotels, bakeries, restaurants, churches, and many cabins and dwellings. The post office was established on October 7, 1851, and by 1852 the camp boasted more than six hundred people.

Up until 1921, when State Highway 49 was extended to Goodyears Bar, the only road access was from the Henness Pass Road, 2,000 feet above the river and four air miles to the south. See the section that describes the Goodyears Bar to Forest City Road. (See page 78 for more detailed information.)

Downieville

Among the first Europeans in the area were Philo Haven and his nephew Carlos, Francis Anderson, Warren Goodall, and Thomas Angus. They located at what came to be known as Little Rich Bar, about one half-mile below present day Downieville, in September of 1849. They discovered gold on September 14.

William Downie, an emigrant from Scotland, reached Sacramento on a schooner on July 5 of 1849. Downie and his party of ten black sailors, an Indian, an Irish boy named Michael Deverney, and a Kanaka (Hawaiian) named Jim Crow, left Sacramento and headed for the Yuba River. They arrived in November at "The Forks," the place where a smaller river joined the North Yuba. Following the smaller river a short ways north, they came upon several men working a little bar just below the Blue Banks, a very rich section of river bed and bank gravels. The party camped for a time on nearby Jersey Flat where they learned they could find gold in the most unusual of places. Tradition has it that one morning, Jim Crow caught a trout weighing between twelve and fourteen pounds, and after cooking it that night for supper, they found gold in the bottom of the kettle. It is reported that during the winter of 1850, close to 5,000 people wintered at the Forks.

Downie and his troop later moved on to Zumwalt Flat where they put up a few log cabins for shelter against the rapidly approaching winter. The party's supplies were already running low, so late in December a party of eight men led by Jim Crow were sent down river for provisions. When the weather allowed those who were still left in camp to work, they were pleasantly surprised to find the area so rich, infact, it was not uncommon for them to make one to two hundred dollars a day. But by late February, the snow put an end to all work on the diggings, forcing the men to remain indoors in their cabins. By March the party that was sent for supplies had not yet returned and the food was nearly gone, so the men were forcced to go on rations. Fortunately, the arrival of spring and the return of Jim Crow with provisions found the men still alive. The Forks soon became the center of a wide circle of camps stretching out in all directions.

With the large number of miners entering the area and so many claims being staked, many disputes arose between claim holders, making it necessary to call a meeting to establish a set of mining laws for the region. The miners had their meeting and adopted a set of rules, one of which limited the size of a claim to thirty feet. After the meeting, things went on smoothly again for some time—until the lawyers arrived on the scene.

On July 5, 1851, "Judge Lynch" sealed the fate of a young lady named Juanita. She had been found guilty of killing Jack Cannon when he insulted her. Justice was swift in Downieville. The murder, trial, and subsequent hanging from the bridge over the Yuba River, all happened on the same day. This wasn't the only execution that would occur. There were murders, robberies, and duels. In fact, the Sheriff's gallows has now been restored and is considered a local landmark.

A miner's life was not a cheap or easy one in Downieville. Supplies had to be brought in over the rough riverside trail, and necessities were both scarce and expensive; a simple wool shirt cost $50, sugar sold for $4 a pound, boots and shoes ran from $25 to $150 a pair. Most of the miner's day was spent knee deep in ice-cold waters, panning, sluicing, or rocking.

On the night of February 19, 1852, Downieville was completely destroyed by fire. The blaze swept through the cloth tents and clap-board shacks leaving rubble and smoldering ashes. Damages were estimated at $150,000 and although many lost everything they owned, the town was quickly rebuilt using more substantial materials and business and life returned to normal. The large population living along the Yuba River, the region's vast wealth, and the fact that the county seat at Marysville was too far away for effective government, prompted the citizens to petition the State legislature to separate a portion of Yuba County and create a new county to be called Sierra. On April 16, 1852, it was done and Downieville became the county seat.

One of the largest gold "nuggets" ever found in the world was reportedly unearthed near Downieville in 1853 by a man known as Finney. The mass of gold weighed 5,009 ounces, contained only a small amount of quartz, and was valued at $84,302. Its shape re-sembled a pair of dumbbells, the link between the two being broken when Finney pried it out of the ground. Taken to San Francisco, the nugget was put on display on the counter of a prominent mercantile firm where it was viewed by thousands before finally being shipped back east.

The town suffered a second disastrous fire on New Year's Day, 1858. Once again the flames were out of control and everything in their path was destroyed, including the bridge to Jersey Flat. As before, the town was rebuilt, although not as quickly. By this time gold had become more difficult to find as the river and its tributaries were finally drying up. The continuing decline of the mining region eventu-ally led to many of the town's citizens leaving the area.

Downieville has changed little since those days (Figure 42). Be sure to visit Cannon Point, just west of town. This twelve hundred pound cannon was first "fired" in 1862 for celebrations.

Figure 42. Downtown Downieville is an adventure into the past. It is truly a part of the "lost Sierra."

Unfortunately, the next year two young officers of the California Volunteers were killed when they improperly loaded the cannon during a celebration.

E Clampus Vitus

One cannot study the history of the gold rush without discussing the E Clampus Vitus (ECV). The "Clampers" as they are known, are a mining-community fraternal organization. They are known for their heavy drinking and rowdiness. They are also known for their "spoofing" of the Masons, Elks, and Odd Fellows, and rituals of these groups.

Joseph Zumwalt is credited with bringing the organization to California. (This is the same Zumwalt that originally pioneered the Henness Pass Road.) He arrived in Sacramento on October 23, 1849. First looking for gold in El Dorado

County, then moving south to Mokelumne Hill in 1850. There is a long-standing debate over which ECV chapter was first, Mokelumne Hill, Sierra City, or Downieville. The general consensus, especially in Downieville, is that Downieville was the first to have an organized chapter. Regardless of what chapter was first, the "clampers" became a force to be reckoned with among the miners. Traveling salesmen often found it difficult to sell their wares in the gold country, unless they were clampers.

As more and more people came west, many traditional fraternal organizations such as the Masons, Elks, and Odd Fellows came along, too. They were apt to be clannish and somewhat disapproving of the rowdy miners they encountered, for they took themselves and their rituals quite seriously. To make fun of the fancy sashes and ornate vests, the Clampers took to cutting tin can lids into odd shapes and pinning them to their own simple vests, most often worn over a bright red union suit. They called this "wearing your tin," a practice that continues to this day, although badges, ribbons, and enameled pins have taken the place of tin can lids.

Entertainment was a cherished commodity in the "diggins," for life was hard, brutal, and frequently short. Rather than add to life's burdens, E Clampus Vitus sought to lighten the mood. They viewed the absurdity of life as something to be cherished, using titles, such as "Noble Grand Humbug," "Roisterous Iscutis," "Grand Imperturbable Hangman," "Clamps Vitrix," and "Royal Gyascutis." Flowery oratory, ribald songs, and practical jokes were much admired. Yet the group was a highly respected, and benevolent organization. For example, when a miner fell ill or died, the group would collect food, money and other items to take to the widow and any orphans who had been left behind, as well as comfort them - especially the widow. Numerous newspaper accounts attest to the Clamper's generosity, such as the time when they braved swollen rivers, snowstorms, and treacherous trails to deliver Christmas gifts to those who would otherwise have had nothing.

The organization all but died out around the turn of the century, but was revitalized in 1931 by a San Francisco historian by the name of Carl Wheat, along with his friends George Ezra Dane and Leon O. Whitsell. (Dane, who most often wrote his signature as "G. Ezra Dane," often claimed the "G" stood for "GeeHosaphat." According to Wheat, the "O" in Whitsell's name was for "Obstreperous.") Wheat had found many references to ECV in his historical research and thought it would be fitting for the commemoration and preservation of a segment of California and U.S. History he feared was being lost.

While in the process of studying the Clampers, he visited Adam Lee Moore of Downieville. Mr. Moore was the last known survivor of the old ECV, and passed on all he remembered of the rites, rituals, traditions, and legends of E Clampus Vitus, providing an invaluable link to the past.

In both California and Nevada they are the largest historical organization dedicated to preserving western and mining history. ECV's "serious" side consists of finding, researching, and dedicating plaques to sites, incidents, and people in Western history that might otherwise be overlooked. They have plaqued hundreds of locations from ghost towns to saloons, bordellos to ranchos, and heroes to madmen. After the dedications, they traditionally have a party, known as a "doin's." Partying is where the organization got its reputation as a "historical drinking society," or a "drinking historical society." Although they do not deny that copious amounts of fermented, distilled, and fortified beverages are occasionally consumed at a "doin's," they are opposed to public displays of intoxication, and insist that members who drink liquor have "a Brother of Sobriety holding the reins" on the ride home.

The pre-requisites for becoming a Clamper are a sense of humor, an interest in Western history, an open mind, and a cast iron stomach. If a man has those qualities, and strikes up a friendship with a Clamper or two, he may find himself taken in to the Ancient and Honorable Order. But one can't simply walk up and say, "Can I be a Clamper?" It is up to the Brethren of ECV to invite prospective members to join. And if a man is asked, he should know that the invitation is only given once. If it is refused, it is never tendered again. But a man of any intelligence and character who is so invited would hardly be likely to turn down such a sign of honor. And remember, as the Brethren of E Clampus Vitus maintain, that Clampers are not made, they're born. Like gold, they just have to be discovered.

Loganville

In 1889, Loganville was the homestead of Luigi Lagomarsino, an immigrant from Italy. The town site is located west of the present day campground.

Sierra City

In the spring of 1850, Philo A. Haven and Joseph Zumwalt ventured up the river to this site. They found plenty of signs that Indians were in the area, but as far as they could tell no prospectors had been there before them. Setting up camp, they began mining the banks and riverbed gravels and were soon joined by other hopeful miners. By the end of the year a small settlement had been established where the town now stands. The jagged granite peaks looming over the town to the north were one of the greatest producers of gold in California.

Known for a short time as the Yuba Buttes, they were re-christened the Sierra Buttes at an early point in the town's existence and have been so called ever since. Gold was discovered in the Buttes the same year. Other discoveries followed and by 1852 the craggy Sierra Buttes were honeycombed with many miles of shafts and tunnels. The quartz taken from the mines was crushed in mule-powered arrastres, twenty of which were scattered about the mountainside. Since many of the mines on the Buttes were over eight thousand feet high, equipment and supplies had to be brought in by mule or dragged in on sleds by men with snowshoes.

The winter of 1852-53 proved to be another harsh one. The snow pack became so deep that it triggered an avalanche, which swept the town clean off the mountain. The disaster was so devastating that the place was deserted for several years. Food was scarce before the avalanche and most of the town's people had moved to warmer climates before the avalanche. Following the destruction of the town, small villages began to appear around the more prosperous lode mines.

The Reis brothers bought the Buttes, or most of them, in 1857. Emigrants from Germany, the brothers first mined in Mariposa and later operated a store in Downieville. After purchasing most of the mines, they then proceeded to develop their holdings on a large scale, which helped re-establish the town of Sierra City. The mines of the Buttes were very rich and quite famous for their large lumps of gold. The Monumental Mine was one of the best for producing incredible nuggets, such as a 1,596-ounce nugget in 1860 and a 1,893 "ouncer" in 1869.

Kentucky Mine

About a mile east of Sierra City you will fine the Kentucky Mine and Museum. It is worth taking the time to stop and visit, because they explain how the gold ore was mined and processed.

Bassetts Station

Located at the junction of State Highway 49 and the Gold Lake Road, Bassetts Station was an important way station in the 1860's. Originally named Hancock House, it was renamed in the 1870 for its new owners, Jacob and Mary Bassett. They became the owners when the Yuba Gap Wagon Road was completed. This new wagon route opened up the gold country of western Sierra County to the farmland of Sierra Valley to the east.

Sardine Lakes/Sand Pond

If you are in the area, you should take the little detour to the north and visit the Sardine Lakes and their view of the Sierra Buttes (Figure 43).

Yuba Pass

Yuba Pass, at 6,708 feet above sea level, was an obstacle to commerce until the Yuba Gap Wagon Road was completed between Sierra Valley and Downieville. The story of its construction is a lesson in politics.

As early as 1859, the people that lived along the North Yuba River

Figure 43. Sardine Lake and the Sierra Buttes.

wanted wagon access to the Sierra Valley and points to the east. Those in Sierra Valley wanted the route so they could sell their wares to those along the river. In 1862 a route over the pass was surveyed and the County funded its construction. It wasn't long before the constructor defaulted on the job because the project was going to cost much more than its budget of $54,000.

Between 1863 and 1870 there were several attempts to fund the project by selling bonds. But this took legislative action and votes of the people. It pitched the people of northern Sierra County who would be hurt by such a route against those that would benefit. During the winter legislative session, the State Legislature passed a bill that required the Board of Supervisors to "order an election on the third Monday of April for the purpose of submitting the question of $20,000 in county bonds for the purpose of building a wagon road from Downieville to Sierra Valley." After several amendments and a vote of the people approving the sale of bonds, the project was launched. By August the contractor began work on the road. In the November 12, 1870 edition of *The Mountain Messenger*, an article stated, "The Wagon Road is nearly completed. A few days more and wagons will come through." On December 3rd the wagon road did open, but it wasn't until October of 1871, eleven months later, that the County officially accepted the road.

Sierraville

This high-Sierra community is located at the junction of State Highways 49 and 89. If you turn northeast on 49, you will be heading toward Loyalton and State Highway 70. If you head south on 89, it will take you to Truckee and Interstate 80.

Plumbago Road

Access to the Plumbago Road and Alleghany is from the Pliocene Ridge Road. The paved road turns south towards Alleghany and the Sixteen-to-One Mine. In Allegany, stay to the left as it winds its way north. Just past the General Store, turn right on Kanaka Creek Road.

Alleghany

The Alleghany Gold District was one of the richest gold-producing districts in Sierra County. It extended from Goodyears Bar south to Minnesota Flat. Take time to drive around this old mining town. Use the quick reference guide to checkout the sites.

Hawaiian sailors (known as "Kanaka") that jumped ship in San Francisco first discovered gold in Alleghany in 1852. The Rainbow and Ireland Mines were in full operation a year later. In 1896, Tom Bradbury found a vain of gold in his backyard that was to become the Sixteen-to-One Mine, the most famous of those in Alleghany. (The gold vain was called "tightner" because it narrowed or tightened as the followed it.) In fact, the Sixteen-to-One Mine holdings would incorporate smaller mines in the area, including the Rainbow Mine. By 1965, the mine had yielded over one million ounces of gold. The mine was in operation off and on, well into the 1990's.

The Sixteen-to-One Mine gets its name from a speech given by William Jennings Bryan, when he was campaigning for President. There was a push to establish a monetary standard. The gold mining interests wanted a gold standard, where the silver mining interests wanted a silver standard. Bryant was pushing for a blend, 16 parts silver to 1 part gold. He lost the race and the country went on a gold standard March 14, 1900.

The road to Plumbago is located at the far end of town. It drops off very quickly as it winds it way down toward Kanaka Creek. There are several mine shafts along the road, so keep a lookout. You will also see the "back side" of the Sixteen-to-One Mine buildings across the creek to the northwest.

At the creek you will see an old bridge just downstream and an old stamp mill just upstream (Figure 44). The road pitches up quickly as it runs to the top of Lafayette Ridge. Right near the top, the road splits…take either fork; the one to the right is not quite as steep.

Once on the ridge top, you will cross the Lafayette Ridge Road. If you take the right trail to the west, it will take you out on the ridge to Oak Flat. This section of the trail is a little rougher than the Plumbago Road. The Lafayette Ridge Road to the northeast will take you along the ridge until it connects with the Henness Pass Road near American Hill.

Figure 44. The bridge over Kanaka Creek.

Plumbago

The town of Plumbago is down off the ridge just over a mile. It consists of a few privately owned buildings off a sharp switchback. The town was built to support the mine that is located a ¼-mile down the hill. The mine is located below the town on a very sharp switchback (Figure 45). Again, it is private property so do not enter without permission.

The road narrows as it drops down the ridge toward the Middle Yuba River (Figure 46). As you reach the river there are the remnants of an old mining camp.

Once you cross the bridge, you will be on the Moores Flat Road, as it winds its way through Black Out and Golconda Ravines. This route

Figure 45. The Plumbago Mine is inactive (but you can picture it in full operation).

will take you back to the pavement on the Graniteville Road near Cherry Hill. If you turn left and go to the east, you will eventually come to Bowman Lake. If you turn right, it will take you down the hill towards Malakoff Diggins State Historic Park.

Figure 46. *The Plumbago Road is a county maintained road, but it gets very narrow as it nears the river.*

Just a very short distance down Graniteville Road, you will find Snowtent Springs off to the north. It is said that the water from this spring is 38-degrees all-year long.

Alleghany Quick Reference

Gold was first mined in the Alleghany area in 1852, when Hawaiian sailors, began placer mining in what is now known as Kanaka Creek. Quartz mining began in 1853 at the German Bar and Ireland mines. The Tightner vein was discovered in 1904. Alleghany is named for Alleghany, Pennsylvania.

(1) Sixteen-to-One Mine – *The name for this mining operation has its roots in a plan for a Presidential candidate. The Sixteen-to-One Mine encompasses several mining claims. Operations were discontinued in 1965. There was a brief opening of the mine in the late 1990's.*

(2) Alleghany Hospital – *Alleghany was a "company town." The only hospital in the area was located on a hill above Main Street.*

(3) Tightner Mansion – *The Tightner Mansion (Figure 47) is located just above the site of the Tightner Mine, at the intersection of Main and Miner Streets.*

(4) Plaza – *The town plaza is a small cul-de-sac east of Main Street. This is the location of the fire station.*

(5) General Store – The general store is located on the north end of Main Street. Just beyond the store is Kanaka Creek Road and the access to the Plumbago Road.

Figure 47. The Tightner Mansion sets just above where the Tightner vain was discovered in 1904.

(6) Cemetery – The community cemetery is located on a small hill above the Sixteen-to-One Mine.

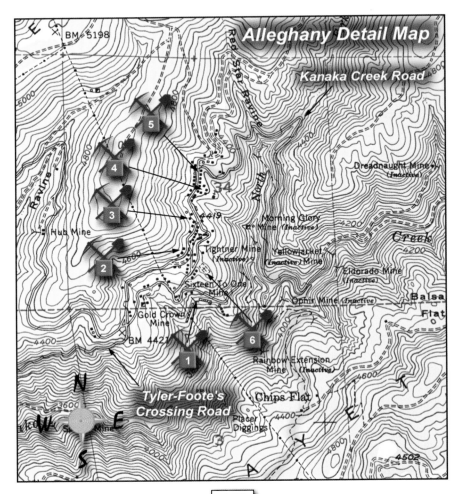

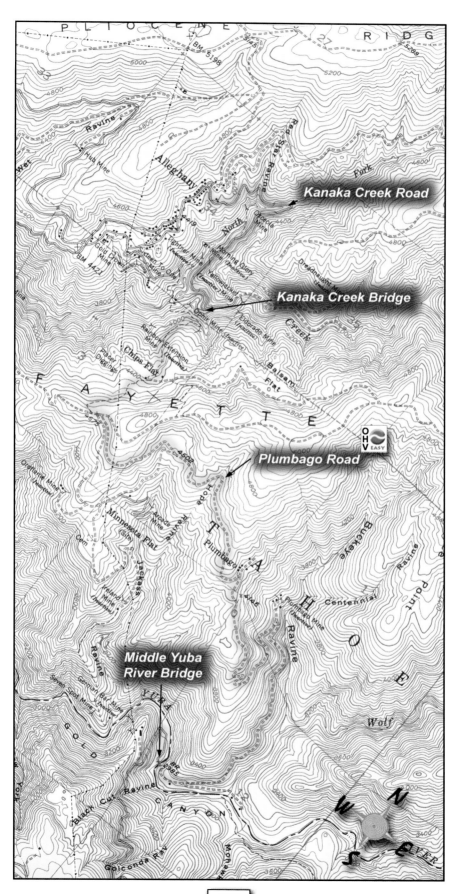

Kanaka Creek Road

Kanaka Creek Bridge

Plumbago Road

Middle Yuba
River Bridge

OHV
EASY

Plumbago Road

Middle Yuba River Bridge

Plumbago, CA

Moores Flat Road

Snowtent Springs

Poker Flat Trail

The trail to Poker Flat is easy (Figure 48). However, there are a couple of loose areas that could cause you some problems when you decide to come out of the area. As you start down the trail, the first landmark will be the access road to the Deadwood Mine.

The trail moves down the ridge toward Canyon Creek and the historic town (site) of Poker Flat. Poker Flat is the name of a placer-mining district that included such claims as Howland Flat, Deadwood, Potosi, and Rattlesnake Peak. It was the site of large hydraulic mining operations from the late 1850's to the 1880's. The name Poker Flat was brought into prominence by author Bret Harte in his book, *The Outcasts of Poker Flat*.

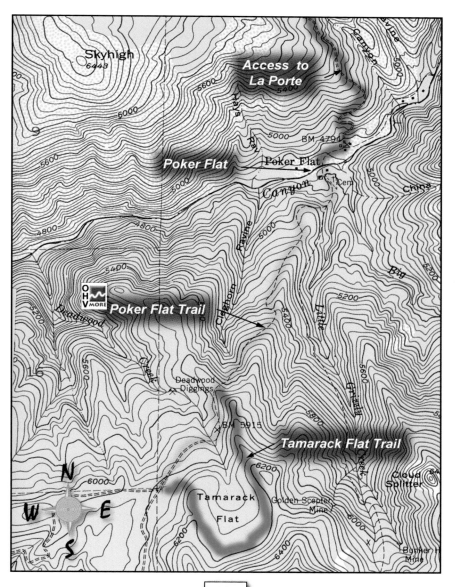

There are a couple of buildings on both sides of the creek. Take time to look around, but remember, this is federally owned land and privately owned mining claims and building. The owners may be very sensitive to trespassers and gold seekers.

Canyon Creek is the boundary between the Tahoe and the Plumas National Forests. If you elect to leave to the north, cross the creek (Figure 49) and head up the ridge. This trail will eventually take you to the community of La Porte and Little Grass Valley Lake.

Figure 48. The trail to Poker Flat is a relative easy one, but there are a couple of loose patches.

Figure 49. The Canyon Creek crossing is easy if the water is low. Poker Flat occupied both sides of the creek, so don't forget to explore those areas to the north.

Red Oak Canyon Trail

The Red Oak Canyon Trail is an "easy" trail, but there are several steep pitches that will require you to use four-wheel drive. The trail is northeast of Downieville, just east of the Craycroft Ridge Trail and north of the Empire Ranch.

Once past the Empire Ranch, you work yourself up Empire Creek. In less than two miles, you will pass the beginning of Craycroft Ridge Trail on your left. As you continue up the bottom of the canyon, you will cross a tributary stream just before you head for the top of the ridge (Figure 50).

As you move up toward the ridge, you will have to negotiate several severe switchbacks. Once on the ridge, the views improve considerably. In about three miles,

Figure 50. The Red Oak Canyon Trail moves through some very dense cover as it moves up the canyon. Once on the ridge, the cover opens up and the views get much better.

the trail forks. The left fork drops off the ridge to the west toward the Gibraltar Mine. The road may be gated before you reach the mine proper.

If you continue north, you will drop down the ridge toward Sunnyside Meadow. On the northwest side of the meadow, there is a nice campsite, protected from the wind, with a good view of Dean's Ravine.

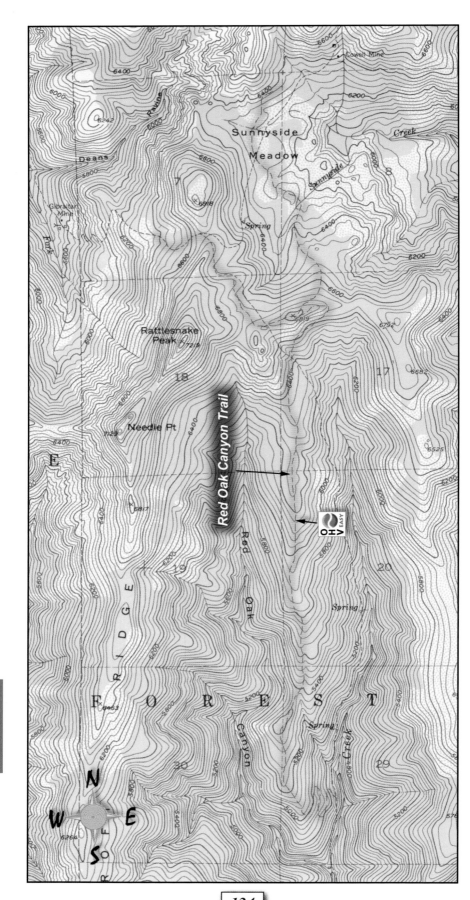

Sierra Buttes Trail

This is a nice easy trail that will take you to the 8,000´ plus summit of the Sierra Buttes, then over the ridge to Packer Saddle. This trail starts in Sierra City. Turn north from Highway 49, at the Mason's Hall onto Butte Street. As you move up the trail, you will see signs of mining activities. In a couple of miles you will come upon the original site of the Sierra Buttes Mine.

Sierra Buttes Mine

The Sierra Buttes Mine is one of the most famous

Figure 51. This small hole next to the tail is the original drift shaft that was to become the Sierra Buttes Mine.

deep quartz mines in the area. It was worked for over a century. There are five separate tunnels in this mine complex. The one just to the right of the trail (Figure 51.) was the first of the shafts. Just as they started digging, they found a pocket of gold that was worth over one million dollars. In 1882, there were four stamp mills (with a total of 96 stamps) working the ore from this mine. In 1888, the mine and milling operation employed just over 200 men that were paid $50 per month.

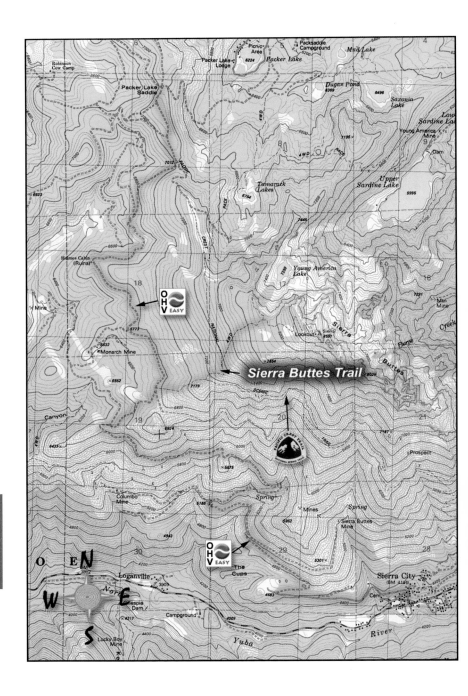

As this historic route continues moving up the ridge it narrows to width of "one wagon" (Figure 52). You will continue to see signs of mining activity until you reach the top of a small ridge. Stay to the right until you see the spur road toward the lookout.

Figure 52. The Sierra Buttes Trail follows the route the miners used over a hundred and fifty years ago.

Sierra Buttes Lookout

The Sierra Buttes Lookout (at 8,591 feet above sea level) is operated by the USDA Forest Service (Figure 53). If you want to visit the lookout, you will have to park and hike a short distance up the hill. It is unstaffed most of the time, so no one may be "home."

Figure 53. The Sierra Buttes Lookout commands an outstanding view of the Gold Lake Recreation Area and the Yuba River Drainage.

Signal Peak Trails

There are two Signal Peak Trails; one that is easy and one that is most difficult. Both lead to Signal Peak, the site of several modern radio and microwave communications facilities. The peak has a history of providing communications, thus it's name.

The Central Pacific Railroad established a "lookout" on this prominent peak to look for fires in the snowsheds. They constructed a stone, two-room building (Figure 54) to provide shelter for their personnel during the harsh winter months. You can still see remnants of the phone line that carried the lookout's reports to the trains below.

Figure 54. Signal Peak has great view of the area. To the south, you can see miles of the railroad and Interstate 80. To the north, you look into Fordyce Creek.

The easiest route begins in Cisco Grove, just north of Interstate 80. The access road turns west for a short distance, before it starts up the mountain to the north. Rattlesnake Road is a well-maintained gravel road. It takes you up the ridge, past the Woodchuck Campground. As you top the grade at Fordyce Summit, the road forks. If you continue straight, and over the ridge, you will reach Fordyce Lake and the Committee Trail; a shortcut to the Fordyce Creek Trail.

If you turn left, you will be heading for Signal Peak. From Fordyce Summit, the trail heads west in a steady climb toward the summit, about 2½-mile and about 1,000 feet in elevation. You will pass a couple of small lakes and a small camping area. As you move up the ridge, you will be able to notice several old mining shafts off to the right. Two that you can see have been closed for

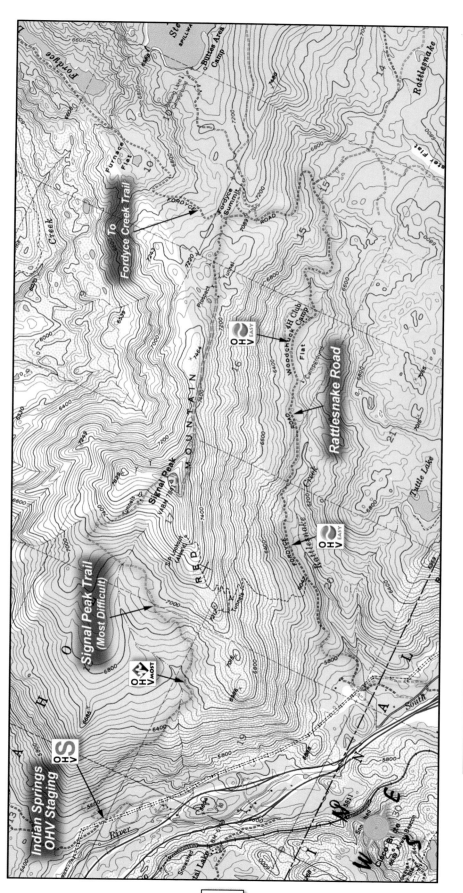

To Fordyce Creek Trail

Rattlesnake Road

Signal Peak Trail
(Most Difficult)

Indian Springs
OHV Staging

years. The water that seeps from them is said to be more acidic than battery acid.

As you reach the top, the road hooks sharply to the right, toward the communication facility. If you look to the left, you will see the railroad hut. Take time to walk the ¼-mile to the hut. When you get there, imagine living there all winter with the snow ten feet deep. Burr!

The most difficult section of the Signal Peak Trail is from the communications facility, down the ridge and slope toward the Indian Springs OHV Staging area. If you elect to take this route back to civilization, you have to work your way around, or over, the various water bars and obstacles. The trail drops down the ridge for about a ½-mile, before it hooks to the left as it drops steeply about 2,000 feet to the river.

If you elect to start your trip on this trail from the bottom, it is accessed from the Indian Springs OHV Staging area. As you enter the staging area, look closely on the right for a narrow track up the hill. The trail moves up the hill steeply (Figure 55). This trail is known for its pitches and wash-outs.

Bob Reed

Figure 55. As you move up the hill, be sure you take time to admire the view.

Snake Lake/Little Deer Lake Trails

The trails to Snake Lake and Little Deer Lake are some of the toughest on the Tahoe National Forest. These trails are rated most difficult because of the pitches between Snake Lake and Oakland Pond, and from Little Deer Lake south to the ridge. In addition, the meadows around these lakes can be damaged very easily, so stay on the historic track.

These trails can be accessed from the Gold Lake Trail, Deer Lake Trail, or from the Gold Valley Trail:

- *Access from Gold Lake and Deer Lake Trails* – *The trail to Snake Lake begins at Summit Lake as it moves up the ridge to the northwest. In less than a mile, the trail to Little Deer Lake turns west. If you continue to the north, the trail will take you to Oakland Pond.*

Oakland Pond – This small lake is a site that was used by Native Americans to rough out basalt tools and arrowheads (Figure 56). All of the basalt chips you will see on the ground are a result

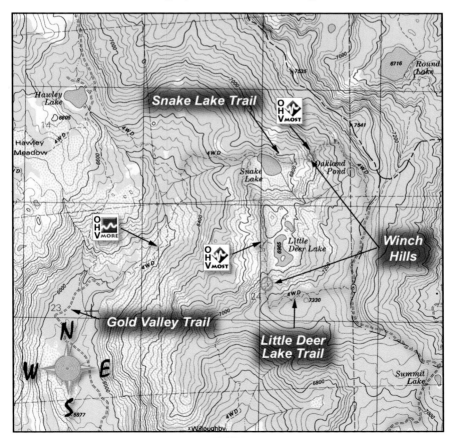

of their actions. On the ridge north of the lake there is a small basalt quarry. This is a great place for lunch.

The trail moves to the north of Oakland Pond. A little further down the trail, it dives off the ridge. To the right is an old mining operation. As you start down the hill, Snake Lake can be seen in the distance (Figure 57). Going down

Figure 56. Oakland Pond is a nice place to have lunch and enjoy the beauty of the area.

this pitch is a lot easier than coming up it. The trail stays to the north of the lake. On the western side of the lake, there is a small campsite. If you continue west, the trail drops down the hill to Gold Valley.

- *Access from Gold Valley Trail – The trail to Snake Lake is just under a mile from Hawley Lake. It is about a ½-mile up the ridge to Snake Lake. If you continue east toward Oakland Pond, you will have a real challenge ahead of you and winching may be in your future.*

Snake Lake – This lake also deserves some time to visit and to picnic or camp.

Figure 57. Snake Lake is a beautiful lake with a nice campsite on the west side of the lake. Note the trail track in the lower left hand corner of the photo.

If you turn south at Snake Lake, you will head up the ridge toward Little Deer Lake (Figure 58). The trail will be rocky and narrow. There are several ledges you will have to negotiate.

Little Deer Lake – This lake sets several hundred feet above Snake Lake (Figure 59). There are several very nice campsites next to the lake. Rumor has it that the fishing is pretty good.

Bob Reed

Figure 58. *The trail between Snake Lake and Little Deer Lake is a steep one.*

The trail continues to the south as it moves up the slope quickly. You may find yourself having to use your winch. At the top of the ridge, the trail hooks sharply east. It is a mile back to Summit Lake.

- *Access to Little Deer Lake from Summit Lake – As you move up the trail from Summit Lake, in about a ½-mile you will reach a fork in the road; take the track to the left. This track*

Figure 59. *Little Deer Lake is a beautiful lake to visit. It is said the fishing is pretty good.*

will meander up the ridge, winding back and forth around trees. It then turns sharply to the right, and starts down the ridge. Just before a real steep pitch, there is a great view of Little Deer Lake and the upper end of Gold Valley.

Tyler-Foote's Crossing Road

The Tyler-Foote's Crossing Road is one of the most scenic wagon roads in the area. It is "easy" and perfect for a day trip in your sport utility vehicle. The recommended direction of travel would be from Alleghany downhill toward North Columbia. The trail starts just west of town at the intersection of Main and Miner Streets.

A. D. Foote, the Superintendent of the Tightner Consolidated Mines in Alleghany, constructed the Tyler-Foote's Crossing Road in 1913 and 1914. Sierra and Nevada counties and the USDA Forest Service provided the funding for the road. Its purpose was to provide an alternate route to Alleghany, which was often snowed-in during winter.

As you move down canyon from Alleghany, you will pass some interesting historical sites. One of the first is the community dump. There are probably a lot of "storys" this place could tell. About two miles from town you will make a sharp hairpin turn to the left...you can still see several fruit trees in the underbrush. This is the site of the Mack House, the local brothel, after it was moved from town.

About five miles from town you will see a road running off toward the creek. This is the road to the Kenton Mine. The mine is no longer active, but the old mine buildings have been turned into a resort.

The Tyler-Foote's Crossing Road works it way down and then out of the Kanaka Creek drainage (Figure 60). There was more gold taken per mile in this creek than any other creek or river in California. It is also completely

Figure 60. Kanaka Creek produced more gold per mile than any other creek or river in California.

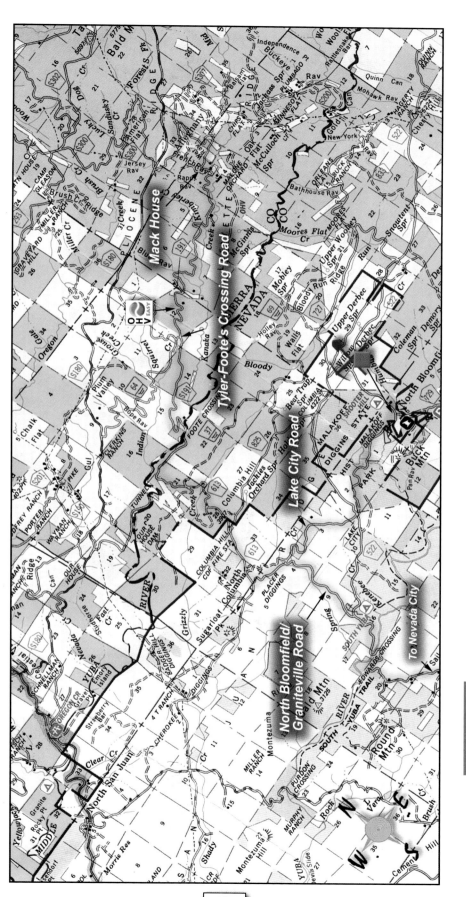

Mack House

Tyler-Foote's Crossing Road

Lake City Road

North Bloomfield/
Graniteville Road

To Nevada City

"claimed." There isn't an inch that you can pan without trespassing on someone's mining claim. Don't risk it…these claims are patrolled.

The two mile section of the road, from the crossing west, is constructed across the face of cliffs…some of them hundreds of feet above Kanaka Creek. Rock walls, literally anchored to the cliff with iron rods, support the roadbed (Figure 61). Rock masons from Italy constructed these rock walls. Take your time moving along this section of the road. Some sections are very narrow. You can take the Tyler-Foote's Crossing Road all the way back to Highway 49.

Figure 61. The roadway is actually constructed on rock walls constructed by rock masons from Italy.

Or, you can take the Lake City Road to the Malakoff Diggins.

Malakoff Diggins

While in the area, take time to visit the Malakoff Diggins State Historical Park. This is the site of the largest hydraulic mining area in California. The North Bloomfield Mining and Gravel Company operated it from 1855 until 1884. The mining operation reached its peak in the 1870's. The diggings were named by French miners in celebration of the capture of Fort Malakoff during the Crimean War in Europe in 1855.

Some of the first miners in the area panned for gold and got nothing but dirt. They said "humbug" for not finding their riches and with that, named the creek they were working Humbug Creek. Two years later, with the advent of hydraulic mining in the region, a town sprang up near the creek, which was called Humbug. As hydraulic mining became more and more prevalent, the town grew and was soon an important mining center for the region.

In an effort to provide better drainage needed to reach the richest deposits, the company embarked on one of the greatest mining engineering feats of all time, carving an eight thousand foot long drainage tunnel through solid bedrock. Hamilton Smith was the engineer in charge of digging the tunnel, and after thirty months of intense activity, he saw his tunnel completed on November 15, 1874. This allowed the company to mine the deep gravels and dump the tailings directly into the South Yuba River. It is said that over 50,000 tons of material was moved each day during its peak operation. The operation used seven giant monitors twenty-four hours a day, seven days a week. These huge nozzles threw water hundreds of feet, washing the material down through a tunnel. The tunnel was lined with "sluice boxes" that separated the gold from the gravel. It probably was not the most efficient way of extracting the gold, but millions of dollars of gold were taken from these hills. The scar created by this operation is roughly 3,000 feet wide, 7,000 feet long and as deep as 600 feet (Figure 62).

Figure 62. The Malakoff Diggins "hole" covers hundreds of acres and is as much as 600 feet deep. Millions of dollars of gold were extracted from these hills between 1855 and 1884.

Sawyer Decision

Hydraulic mining proved not to be very profitable, and it was devastating to the environment. The waste of gravel, mud, and water from the mining operations were initially dumped into Humbug Creek and later into the Yuba River. At Marysville, debris from the Malakoff mine choked the Yuba River until the river bottom was higher than the town, causing severe flooding and damage. And as the bed of the Sacramento River rose, floods struck the rich agricultural areas in California's great Central Valley, resulting in millions of dollars in damages for local farmers.

The farmers, who were not about to let hydraulic mining destroy their land, fought back and by June 1883 the case was being heard in the courtroom of Judge Lorenzo Sawyer. A Marysville property owner named Woodruff had brought suit against the North Bloomfield Gravel Mining Company to stop them from dumping "tailings" into the Yuba River. In January 1884, Sawyer handed down his decision, ruling in favor of the farmers. This was the famous Sawyer Decision, *the first environmental legislation in the United States*, and the decision that effectively brought an end to the era of hydraulic mining in California.

North Bloomfield

When the post office was established in 1857, the residents of Humbug felt their town needed a better name, so they decided to vote on the matter. Bloomfield was the people's choice, to which the post office added "North" to distinguish it from Bloomfield in Sonoma County.

North Bloomfield prospered greatly due mainly to the highly productive Malakoff Mine, and claimed some seventeen hundred residents, which included a large settlement of Chinese immigrants. To provide for the needs of its citizens and visitors, the town offered eight saloons, five hotels, three lodging houses, two dry goods stores, two grocery stores, two breweries, two livery stables, two churches, a barbershop, a blacksmith, a butcher, a baker, a school, a post office, and daily stage and freighting service.

Today the ghost town of North Bloomfield and the nearby Malakoff mine are within the boundaries of the three thousand acre Malakoff Diggins State Historic Park. Several of the town's original buildings are still standing, while a few others have been reconstructed to their original designs. A museum contains bits and pieces of the town's history and the Ranger's office can usually answer visitor's questions. The park also contains picnic and camping grounds, and numerous trails that wander through the mountains, lakes, streams and diggings. Blair Lake, originally a reservoir for the mines, offers a beautiful spot for a picnic and is furnished with tables and barbecues.

Appendix

USDA Forest Service

Tahoe National Forest
Supervisor's Office
631 Coyote Street
Nevada City, CA 95959
(530) 265-4531
www.r5.fs.fed.us/tahoe/

Downieville Ranger District
15924 Highway 49
Camptonville, CA 95922
(530) 288-3231

Foresthill Ranger District
22830 Foresthill Road
Foresthill, CA 95631
(530) 367-2224

Nevada City Ranger District
631 Coyote Street
Nevada City, CA 95959
(530) 265-4531

Sierraville Ranger District
Highway 89/PO Box 95
Sierraville, CA 96126
(530) 994-3401

Truckee Ranger District
10342 Highway 89 North
Truckee, CA 96161
(530) 587-3558

Big Bend Visitor Info Center
49685 Hampshire Rocks Road
Soda Springs, CA 95728
(530) 426-3609

Plumas National Forest
Supervisor's Office
159 Lawrence Street
Quincy, CA 95971
(530) 283-2050

Other Important Contacts

Tread Lightly!, Inc.
298 24th Street, Suite 325
Ogden, UT 84401
(801) 627-0077

Forest City Museum
(530) 287-3413

CA Association of 4WD Clubs, Inc.
8120 36th Avenue
Sacramento, CA 95824
(916) 381-8300

Bibliography

_____, *Kyburz Flat 2000 Years of History*, USDA Forest Service, 1994.

_____, *Forest City—Historic Walking Tour*, USDA Forest Service, 1999.

_____, *From Gold to Silver—The Comstock Connection: A Historic Driving Tour of the Henness Pass Road*, USDA Forest Service, 1999.

Byrd, David S., *Roads and Trails in the Tahoe National Forest: A Contextual History, 1840 – 1940*, USDA Forest Service, 1992.

Florin, Lambert, *Ghost Towns of the West*, Promontory Press, 1971.

Graydon, Charles K., *Trail of the First Wagons Over the Sierra Nevada*, The Patrice Press, Tucson, AZ, 1986.

Hinkle, George and Bliss, *Sierra-Nevada Lakes*, University of Nevada Press, Reno, NV, 1987.

Johnson, William Weber, *The Forty-Niners*, Time-Life Books, New York, 1974.

Lawler, David, *Ancestral Yuba River Gold Map*, California Gold Publications, Berkeley, CA, 1995.

Letham, Lawrence, *GPS Made Easy*, The Mountaineers, Seattle, WA, 1998.

Jackson, W. Turrentine, *History of Tahoe National Forest 1840-1940*, USDA Forest Service, 1982.

McGlashan, C. F., *History of the Donner Party*, Stanford University Press, Stanford, CA, 1940.

Nordhoff, Charles, *The Central Pacific Railroad*, Vistabooks, Silverthorne, CO, 1996.

Rose, James J., *Sierra Trailblazers First Pioneer Wagons Over The Sierra Nevada*, Lake Tahoe Historical Society, 1995.

Shinn, Charles Howard, *Mining Camps A Study in American Frontier Government*, Harper Torchbooks, New York, 1965.

Sinnott, James J., *Downieville Gold Town on the Yuba*, The California Traveler, Volcano, CA, 1972.

Sinnott, James J., *History of Sierra County, Volume III, Alleghany and Forest City*, The California Traveler, Volcano, CA, 1975.

Wheeler, Keith, *The Railroaders*, Time-Life Books, New York, 1973.

Zauner, Phyllis and Lou, *California Gold Story of the Rush to Riches*, Zanel Publications, Sonoma, CA, 1997.

Index

Ordering Information

If you would like to order additional copies of this or other products from Deer Valley Press, you can contact Deer Valley Press several different ways:

Telephone: (530) 676-7401 or (800) 455-1950.
Facsimile: (530) 676-7418
EMail: dvp@deervalleypress.com
Mail: 5125 Deer Valley Road, Rescue, CA 95672

You can pay for products using personal check, VISA, MASTERCARD, money orders, purchase orders, or if you represent a business, we will provide an invoice that can be used to make payment.

Order Form

	Number	Unit Price	Total
4 Wheeler's Guide - Trails of the San Bernardino Mtns.		*$19.95*	
4 Wheeler's Guide - Trails of the Tahoe National Forest		*$19.95*	
4 Wheeler's Guide to the Rubicon Trail		*$19.95*	

SALES TAX (CA residents add 7.00%)

SHIPPING (Add $4 for the first Guide and $1.00 for each additional.

TOTAL

Ship to:

Name   Telephone Number

Address

City   State   Zip Code

Credit Card Information

Credit Card Number

Circle the card used.

MasterCard   VISA

Cardholder's Name   Exp. Date

Signature